FAMILY AND COMMUNITY FUNCTIONING

A Manual of Measurement
for Social-Work Practice
and Policy

*Second, revised, and
expanded edition*

LUDWIG L. GEISMAR

The Scarecrow Press, Inc.
Metuchen, N.J., & London
1980

The first edition of
Family and Community Functioning
was printed in 1971 by Scarecrow Press.

Library of Congress Cataloging in Publication Data

Geismar, Ludwig L
  Family and community functioning.

  Bibliography: p.
  Includes index.
  1. Family social work--Evaluation. 2. Social
service. I. Title.
HV43.G45 1980 362.8'2'0287 80-17785
ISBN 0-8108-1332-7
ISBN 0-8108-1341-6 paper

Acknowledgments

Social-science endeavors seldom spring full blown from un-tilled soil. Typically they build upon the work of many others who have given thought to the same problem. This is particularly true of the effort before us. The instrument for measuring family functioning that is described here is actually a revised version of one of the research products of the Family Centered Project of St. Paul, a pioneer undertaking dating back to the late 1940s; the goal of which was to serve what came to be known as the multiproblem family. The present work is based on my collaboration in the Project with Beverly Ayres, whose premature death deprived the field of social work of an exceedingly able researcher.

I am most grateful to Charles J. Birt, former Director of the Family Centered Project and the United Fund and Councils of St. Paul, Minnesota, for permission to reproduce sections of the earlier manual, entitled *Measuring Family Functioning* (1960).

To Professor Ursula Gerhart of Rutgers University, formerly Associate Director of the Family Life Improvement Project, I am particularly indebted. She assisted greatly in the development of the Community Functioning Scale and the instrument for the Self-Evaluation of Family Functioning. Professor Gerhart also took charge of the fieldwork in which these tools underwent their first test, and of the family-functioning coding operation, which led to improvements in measurement procedure.

A special vote of thanks goes to Harriet Fink, Research Associate in the Family Life Improvement Project, for doing the computer work required by this study and for assisting most ably in coding and other aspects of data analysis. To the conscientious and dedicated coding team, composed of Harriet Fink, Judy Schwartz, Zona Fishkin, Patricia Lagay, and Dorothy Jaker, my hearty thanks. Special recognition is due to Professor Isabel Wolock, Associate Director of the Rutgers Social Work Research Center, and to Professor Bruce Lagay, formerly Assistant Director of the Family Life Improvement Project, for aiding this effort in innumerable ways. I am furthermore indebted to my Methods in Social Work Research class of 1969, fall semester, for subjecting the Community Functioning Scale to a reliability test-retest and a field test in the community. Thanks also go to Professor Dingley and his students in the Community Organization class of the summer, 1970, for participating in the test-retest.

I owe a debt of gratitude to the U.S. Social Rehabilitation

Service for its support of the Family Life Improvement Project
(HEW Grant Number 190), from which some of these data were
taken. I am also indebted to the Rutgers University Research
Council for a faculty fellowship that allowed me to devote time
to writing, and to Professor Werner Boehm, the former Dean of
the Rutgers Graduate School of Social Work, for temporarily
freeing me from teaching responsibilities and giving encouragement in these and related efforts.

Finally, very special thanks go to my wife Shirley for help
with the collection of family and community data and for
extensive and creative editorial assistance.

Table of Contents

Preface to the Second Edition

Nine years have passed since the publication of the first edition of *Family and Community Functioning*. This is a long period in view of the accelerated development in social-work research technology during the 1970s. Social workers and members of the other helping professions may take pride in the fact that recent efforts of researchers aimed at enlarging the scientific base of the profession have produced a number of instruments and models of measurement that possess a good potential for furthering the research goals. This development places the endeavors reported in this volume into a broader context of methodology designed to evaluate professional social-work services.

A further reason for issuing a revised and expanded version of *Family and Community Functioning* is the wish to acquaint the reader with several modifications of the measurement techniques described in the 1971 edition. The changes are the result of the continued application of both scales in this country and abroad. The last two chapters in particular have benefited from empirical research done since this book was first published.

I. Introduction

The juxtaposition of family and community in a manual on measurement may seem strange at first glance, since the two concepts represent social systems that differ widely in size, life span, internal variability, purpose, goals, and a variety of other dimensions. Even sociological theorists, forever eager to build on common theoretical foundations, have found it necessary to start their theorizing about family and community from different vantage points. Why should anyone insist, then, on covering such diverse subject matter within the limited space of a small volume?

1

The answer lies outside the context of conceptual similarity. It derives mainly from the need of social-work practice to address itself simultaneously or in close succession to the performance, problems, practices, and policies of both family and community. This dual focus in practice requires a parallel approach in research, if research is to play an effective part in the solution of problems encountered in the field.

The reciprocal relationship between family and community is well illustrated in the controversy that raged during the mid-sixties over the use of the concept *multiproblem family*. Responding to a flood of speeches and articles describing the characteristics of the multiproblem family, a number of writers, concerned with the functioning of the welfare system, pointed to its serious shortcomings and the reciprocal relationship between family and community problems. They believed, in effect, that the term *multiproblem agency* or *community* better characterized the problem situation.

While the nature of the foregoing controversy represents a polemic that cannot be resolved by logical means, there are nonetheless some basic truths contained in the argument that community and family problems are interdependent. The relationships between disease and absence of medical service, or between poverty and lack of employment or financial-aid programs, have been well documented. In a similar vein, the histories of multiproblem families generally reveal a pattern of agency failure to provide adequate and continuing service to those who cannot make it on their own.

The emergence and development of subdisciplines— variously referred to as practice methods or areas of concentration—within American social work reveal a spreading of concern from microsystems, such as the individual and the family, to macrosystems, such as the municipal, state, and national welfare systems. Social casework, the first practice method to emerge as a full-fledged professional discipline, has increasingly advocated that its service focus be extended from

the individual to the nuclear family to kinship and neighborhood groupings. Group work, community organization, administration, and social policy—the social-work subdisciplines
that emerged in the wake of social casework—broadened their
intervention foci to successively larger social systems. Their
development within the framework of the same profession provides testimony of a belief shared by professionals that the
interrelatedness of conditions, behavior, functioning, problems, needs, and wants calls for a joining of efforts in dealing
with all of them.

Such cooperation may occur either at the planning level, in
the formulation of programs, or at the practice level, where
services may need to be coordinated in order to reach given
objectives. Attempts to relate problems of practice from two or
more areas on intervention by means of joint theorizing, research planning, and evaluation are relatively rare in social
work. Yet joint approaches aimed at determining the interrelationship of conditions, problems, and practices are the key to
the growth of a unified, science-based profession.

The present monograph seeks to initiate efforts to integrate
practice at the family and community levels by way of assessing patterns of social functioning, seeing conceptualization and
measurement as first, but necessary, steps in attaining the
more ambitious goals outlined above.

This manual is written mainly as a how-do-it book for the
research practitioner. A discussion of the theoretical underpinnings of measurement precedes the presentation of instruments and their use. For the sake of compactness, reliability
and validity studies and other methodological endeavors, such
as there are, are cited but not presented in full. The interested
reader is encouraged to refer to the sources for a fuller treatment of each respective subject.

The family-functioning scale is a modified version of that
presented about two decades ago as part of the St. Paul Family
Centered Project, while the community-functioning scale rep-

resents the fruits of more recent efforts by the author. Neither instrument is presented as the last word in its respective kind of measurement. On the contrary, like all instruments of social and psychological measurement these scales must be viewed in the context of the population, social structure, service patterns, and research goals. Past applications furnish guidelines for future use or limitations to such use. Like other tools of measurement in the social and behavioral sciences, the instruments presented here need to be considered against possible alternatives for attaining study objectives.

The scales for measuring family and community functioning are designed for the systematic collection and analysis of data useful to the researcher and practitioner in both the policy and direct-service fields. Because of their broad scope and comprehensive nature, the instruments lend themselves to specification and elaboration in data collection as suggested by the foci of given programs of service. Instrument modification, it should be stressed, is nonetheless a task for an investigator who has acquired a measure of methodological sophistication. Whether the methods of evaluation presented here are employed as shown in this book or modified to meet the needs of given projects, this writer hopes that the present volume will stimulate efforts toward practice that is guided by the use of meaningful and valid family and community welfare data.

II. Standardized Evaluation
in Social Work:
A Brief Perspective

The theme of systematic evaluation in social work goes back to the early 1900s, as Zimbalist (pp. 233–237) has shown, although during the first two thirds of the century evaluation research could best be described as the isolated efforts of a few scholars and research organizations. During the past decade the evaluative-research movement gathered considerable strength, reflecting the growing influence of a scientific school of thought in social-work education and the mounting pressures emanating from government and other public bodies for service accountability. Over four dozen social-work outcome studies have been subjected to the scrutiny of critical reviewers (Fischer 1973, 1976; Geismar 1971; Grey and Dermody; Gurman 1973, 1974; Hollis; Mullen and Dumpson; Segal; Wood).

The first wave of outcome studies in the direct-service field yielded a variety of conclusions ranging from negative results denoting no significant improvement as the result of the experiment (Berleman, Seaberg, and Steinburn; Meyer, Borgatta, and Jones; Mullen, Chazin, and Feldstein; Wallace) to positive findings indicating significant change in the desired direction (Beck and Jones 1973; Behling; Geismar 1968; Schwartz and Sample). The predominant type of result of the systematic-evaluation studies done in the 1950s and 1960s is one of limited but statistically nonsignificant gains resulting from the services rendered.

Given this skeptical assessment of the state of the art, the need to explain apparent failure took mainly two forms. One position, exemplified by Fischer (1973) and Segal, questioned the effectiveness of the intervention measured, especially casework. A more analytic stance, illustrated by the writings of Beck and Jones (1974) and Wood, pointed to the network of factors interacting to produce negative results. These include inappropriate (in some cases) techniques of service, unsuitable research design, and insensitive measures of outcomes.

The emergence of different patterns of evaluation research may be attributed largely to the predominantly negative findings of the studies reported and to the criticisms leveled against them. The basic problem as seen by a number of writers (Fischer 1978, pp. 88-136; Hudson 1978; Thomas; Wood, pp. 454-456) hinges on the choice of research models for evaluating social-work programs. The relevancy of the experimental design for studying the effects of services was put in doubt, and a number of alternative models, including the R and D approach (Thomas); N=1 model (Howe; Jayaratne 1977,

1978); and problem-focused techniques (Beck and Jones 1974, p. 599; Kiresuk and Sherman; Reid and Epstein 1972) were aired in the research literature.

A balanced assessment of the results of social work does not reveal a picture of ineffectiveness but a range of outcomes whose relationship to such factors as type of service and methods of evaluation remains, for the time being, a matter of conjecture (Geismar 1971; Wood). Surveys of intervention in such cognate disciplines as psychotherapy (Bergin and Garfield; Smith and Glass) and marital counseling (Beck 1975) yielded a balance sheet of outcomes more favorable than that derived from the evaluations of social-work programs. The difference, one might assume, is at least partly due to the much larger volume of research in these related fields. More sharply focused measurement in the latter, particularly in the area of behavior therapy, may also account for the proportionately greater frequency of positive outcomes.

The notion of focused measurement in social work has its origin in the so-called problem-centered approaches to evaluation described by Zimbalist (pp. 253–257) and illustrated in the studies of Reed (1931) and Heckman (1948). The central idea in problem-centered evaluation is the contention that services are designed to alleviate problems presented by clients and that service effectiveness can best be gauged by whether or not these problems have been relieved as a result of the service.

This thesis is clearly defensible as long as intervention itself is clearly problem focused. Such is not invariably the case, despite the fact Helen Perlman, a leading casework theorist, termed it "a problem-solving process" (Perlman, pp. 27–39). It must be kept in mind that social casework that builds on ego psychology views the client's problem as a multifaceted dynamic construct in which cause and effect interact. Under this formulation the salient casework goals are couched in language that denotes coming to grips with the underlying causes of the client's difficulties, such as lack of motivation for help and insufficient emotional and intellectual capacity to use services and cope with problems. Intervention, therefore, is directed toward an understanding of self, a strengthening of client ego, including his or her motivation and capacity for dealing with problems, and a general improvement in psychosocial functioning. These goals do not obviate the need for dealing with tangible client problems—these need to be addressed, with priority given to the most urgent ones—but it subordinates them to the more fundamental as well as global casework goals such as were identified above.

It is no accident then that the first scientifically validated instrument for measuring the effects of casework, the Hunt-Kogan Scale, developed at the Community Service Society of New York, pinpointed the theoretically relevant (to ego psychology) dimensions of verbalized attitudes and understanding, disabling habits and conditions, adaptive efficiency, and environmental circumstances as criteria of change or movement in the client (Hunt and Kogan, pp. 30–38). Except for the last category, material circumstances, the Hunt-Kogan Scale groupings single out client behavior and attitudes as the criteria by which the effectiveness of professional intervention is to be judged.

Leaving aside the philosophical question of what should be the proper concern of social work, some advantages come to mind as being more inherent in the more global (or less focused—Coulton and Solomon [1977] make the distinction between "generalized" and "individualized") type of measures, such as the Hunt-Kogan Scale. It addresses itself to the more lasting aspects of client functioning, namely those that presumably are more stable than are the client's problems and yet highly correlated with the latter. The measure may also be said to provide a more balanced and hence diagnostically useful picture of behavior. A further advantage of the Hunt-Kogan method lies in its greater compatibility with a preventive approach to helping, because evaluation is not dependent on a degree of problem incidence or prevalence in order to make measurement possible. However, the salient consideration for those advocating the use of a generalized measure such as the Hunt-Kogan Scale is its theoretical relevance to the treatment program.

The disadvantages of the more global technique, as already indicated, include the lack of focus that is likely to identify minor changes in the life of the client. This argument could be countered by stating that the overall service goal—related relevancy of measurement—supercedes a desire to demonstrate client movement. Put differently, it may be questioned whether showing evidence of change is indeed such a desirable thing if the change has not taken place in those dimensions of client behavior that are the target of intervention.

At this point the argument does return to the fundamental question of treatment philosophy. Intervention programs stressing modifying, also referred to as "reconstructive" techniques (Reid and Shyne, p. 21), aimed at basic changes in personality and interpersonal relations, can be differentiated prescriptively from those that stress problem solving or supportive functions. A case can surely be made for giving precedence of one over the other, and the field of social-work direct service has been split on this subject. Complicating the theoretical issue, however, is the finding from a couple of studies, which have examined the subject empirically, that differences in treatment philosophy do not properly reflect the differences in intervention techniques (Reid and Shyne, pp. 90-95). Regardless of orientation, such casework services that have undertaken to identify treatment techniques tend to give priority to an exchange of information regarding the client's problems rather than dealing with intrapsychic causation and development (Reid and Shyne, p. 91; Geismar, Lagay, et al., pp. 134-138). It would follow that a recognition that social-work direct service invariably addresses itself to the problems burdening the client should lead to a highlighting of the problem focus in the evaluation of outcome.

A problem-centered evaluation approach that is closely

linked to the treatment modality is task-centered casework
(Reid and Epstein, 1972, 1977). As a sequel to the research
project by Reid and Shyne, which suggested that planned,
short-term services can yield positive results, Reid and Epstein
tested a model of intervention comprising a "set of procedures
for alleviating explicit target problems perceived by clients"
(Epstein, p. 3). The task-centered model is atheoretical or,
stated perhaps more accurately, not associated with any formal
theoretical framework of human behavior, although the authors believe that it is compatible with any theory or a combination of them that help explain the client's situation (Epstein,
p. 5). Epstein's claim that "task-centered practice is a first line
intervention that will suffice for most situations" is difficult to
validate and certainly has not been subjected to any test in
which the tasks confronting the caseworker vary substantially
from those encountered generally in family-service or public-
welfare agencies. But regardless of the precise scope of application in social work, the task-centered approach represents a
mode of evaluation that avoids the gap, found in some other
approaches, between intervention activities and criteria for
measuring results.

The research of Beck and Jones (1973) also illustrates the
use of problem-centered measurement, applied in this case to a
large sample of clients. This study, however, because of its
scope and the dispersion of study cases over a whole continent,
offered only a limited opportunity to fit the evaluation to mode
of intervention. The researchers, in fact, had no control over
the planning or execution of treatment, but they were in the
unique situation of being able to measure the results of services on a nationwide basis. And the report format, which
utilized a problem framework of client behavior, proved to be a
sensitive measure of change related to treatment.

Perhaps the most highly focused among the problem-
centered approaches to evaluation is goal-attainment scaling
(Kiresuk and Sherman; Kiresuk and Lund). In contrast to

assessment in task-centered casework, goal-attainment scaling is not attached to any particular mode of intervention but designed to fit pragmatically any number of such techniques. This is accomplished by having the researcher identify the treatment goals and specify for each action the levels of attainment desired by the agency or program. This flexibility, though a potential source of strength because it makes the measure applicable to a large variety of service programs, carries with it also the distinct hazard of subjectivity inherent in the mandate of goal setting.

It is hoped that this brief summary of approaches to evaluative measurement in direct services has helped to put across the point that there is not one best method of evaluation. The choice needs to be made in terms of the nature of the intervention, the kind of theoretical framework underlying the program, and the choice of service goals. Problem-centered evaluation is most suited for gauging the immediate effects related to focused forms of intervention. The more global types of assessment are more likely to register diffuse influences, going beyond a single form of service, and more long-range program effects. Behavior-therapy frameworks are more compatible with problem-focused measurements, while psychodynamic orientations call for evaluations that register changes in personality and attitudes.

The St. Paul Scale of Family Functioning as a measure of direct-service outcome belongs to the more global types of instruments. Although the construct of problem functioning is inherent in its conceptual framework, the basic norms for evaluation are functions and roles regardless of whether or not they are problematic. Assessment of change and outcome are guided by cultural (or subcultural) norms applied to socially expected functions. A family's functioning is, therefore, not the sum total of problem behavior or malfunctioning but the balance of adequate as well as marginal and inadequate task and role performance. This approach permits an assessment of strengths as well as weaknesses, covering areas that are not necessarily affected by a specific kind of intervention. More problem-centered evaluation can be carried out, of course, by measuring only those areas of family functioning that are relevant to the intervention.

The more global method of evaluation, represented by the St. Paul Scale, is the most suitable measurement alternative when the research focus is not only on change but also on status (at a point in time) of social functioning and when information is being gathered pertaining to the effects of several programs of intervention or the impact of broad policies as well as sociohistoric forces upon family life. This point will be elaborated further in subsequent chapters.

Evaluative research in social work and social welfare was not from its inception focused on the behavior of individuals and families. Taking their cue from Booth (1902) and Rowntree (1904), the English pioneers in poverty research, the early social-work researchers in this country were primarily interested in the incidence and causes of poverty and deviant behavior. This research interest coincided, of course, with the social reform theme in social work at the turn of the century and the subsequent two decades (Axinn and Levin, pp. 115–136). Early efforts at systematic measurement are well illustrated by the Pittsburgh Survey (Kellogg), which was the most widely publicized effort of the so-called Social Survey Movement. This movement gave impetus to an expanded data-collection activity, which Zimbalist (pp. 181–231) termed "statistics and index making in social work."

The major effort in the field of index making was represented by the social-breakdown studies of the late 1930s and early 1940s. The goal of these studies was the measurement and control of social breakdown, defined as "behavior that does not conform to currently accepted concepts of satisfactory social adjustment" (Zimbalist, p. 227). The social-breakdown index was meant to be used as a gauge of both social need and effectiveness of social service. A basic weakness of this approach was its reliance on official statistics, which at best provided only a crude measure of a population's problems and need and at worst yielded information that told more about the malfunctioning of the community systems (economic, health, welfare, correctional) than the needs of the population surveyed.

The breakdown studies, nonetheless, gave rise to manifold efforts, often quite sophisticated, to measure social need at the community level, and they can properly be viewed as forerunners to the social indicator movement (Bauer; Sheldon and Moore), which at the time of this writing is still gaining momentum. Social-breakdown research also inspired community-action endeavors, such as the St. Paul Family Centered Project by way of community caseload analysis (Buell).

Among efforts to pinpoint the scope of population need of health and welfare services, the priority of needs studies that were conducted in many U.S. communities during the 1950s and early 1960s deserves mention. It was, in fact, the involvement of this writer in one of these research efforts that led him to develop the community-functioning scale presented here. The priority of needs studies used community leaders as judges or raters to rank-order the presumed needs of local populations. This method was based on one of two rather questionable assumptions, namely: (1) *the views of planners and consumers of services coincide, and those of the former are a perfect index of need* (for a test of this notion see Geismar and Lagay); and (2) *if the views differ, the local leadership is in the best position to decide on service and program needs because of its superior expertise on the subject of community need.*

Most of the research technology used in social work for assessing the need for and effectiveness of services is drawn from cognate fields, such as sociology, psychology, urban planning, and public administration. The social-indicator approach, referred to above, represents a potentially powerful tool for problem and need assessment, although its reliance on available statistics sets the limits of effectiveness relative to the quality of these statistics.

The community-functioning measurement presented here uses new data collected from representative samples of the population. It rates the adequacy of services and resources relative to perceived need, thereby obviating the necessity for a separate assessment of problems and needs. This measure of community functioning represents, in fact, an evaluation of the existing services and programs by the actual or potential consumers of services. As an indicant of a family's perspective on the quality of community services the Community Functioning Scale furnishes data on the family-community relationships that supplement the family-functioning profile generated by the St. Paul Scale.

III. The Relevancy of Assessing Family and Community Functioning for Social-Work Intervention

The family and community are the main arena for the planning and delivery of social-work services. This statement does not run counter to the observation that the practice methods of social work, particularly administration and policy, extend their knowledge and skills beyond the community boundaries to the management of services at state, national, and sometimes international levels. But the point of gravity of American programs and services is the home and the community. The community, however defined (more about this later), is the physical and social space in which an individual or family resides, identifies with to some extent, interacts with others, transacts business, spends leisure time, has social and instrumental needs met. Not all of these apply to every person or family because of the complexity and overlapping nature of American communities (some people live in one community, work in a second, and shop in a third), but some of the characteristics identified, particularly residence and receipt of services, apply to all residents of a community.

A proper assessment of the social functioning of the family and the community in which it lives represents a meaningful index of population well-being. This approach affords an opportunity to bring people's welfare and the services designed for them (or their absence) into juxtaposition. The approach used here does not make any assumptions about the quantity and quality of services that should go to any population. Instead, the evaluation of services and programs is seen entirely within the context of need for them. Where such need is absent in one or several areas, the lack of corresponding services is, of course, not measured as a deficit in community functioning. Community malfunctioning in the true sense represents a situation in which important needs of individuals and families are not met.

There is a large gap between accepting the rationale for systematic evaluation and institutionalizing it as a regular component of practice. Since the 1950s the social-work periodic literature has been exhorting researchers and administrators to abandon *ad hoc* and intuitive approaches to the evaluation of practice and to substitute, instead, efforts at objective, systematic assessment. In the 1960s, as a result of a growing belief that the scientific component needed strengthening, and also in response to the prodding of granting agencies (especially those fighting the War on Poverty), efforts at systematic evaluation were greatly stepped up, and published studies tended to replace exhortations. A symposium, planned for January 1971 and sponsored by the Fordham University School of Social Services, was set up to review the findings of studies on the effectiveness of professional intervention in social work. It was able to identify thirteen well-planned and well-executed projects, as well as dozens of others that, in one form or another, fell short of meeting minimum standards of scientific inquiry (Mullen and Dumpson). A thorough review of the literature by Wood covering the period of 1956 to 1973 identified twenty-two studies as having met minimum criteria of scientific rigor (Wood 1978).

A national conference on family measurement, called in 1966 in Washington, D.C., by the Welfare Administration (later Social and Rehabilitation Service) of the U.S. Department of Health, Education, and Welfare, identified the lack of adequate instruments of measurement as a major reason for the dearth of evaluative research (Chilman, p. 4). The conference encouraged efforts to develop appropriate research tools, calling this a necessary first step in the evaluation of social services. This writer tends to share the view expressed by the Washington conference, believing that the number of far-reaching efforts, such as those registered by the Fordham Symposium, would be much greater were this shortage to be alleviated.

Although the number of practitioners who have to be sold on the need for evaluation research is decreasing, there was still in the late 1970s a formidable amount of resistance or indifference to the idea. While this writer cannot cite an exhaustive list of reasons for this position, it is possible to identify a few major roadblocks. Perhaps the main reason social welfare does not feel impelled to evaluate its own product is that welfare agencies and institutions enjoy a monopolistic position (Bredemeier). They do not compete for clients. The picture is, in fact, quite the opposite; social services are very scarce, and potential clients must assert themselves in order to be accepted for treatment. In public agencies complex bureaucratic procedures, preceding the actual service and discouraging their use, are the norm. Private agencies limit admissions with the aid of a waiting list. Survival and growth of the organization do not depend greatly on the quality of service rendered. As a rule, accrediting and evaluation procedures by professional and sponsoring bodies are not rigorous and provide no test of the agency's effectiveness.

Consequently, social agencies feel little need to evaluate their services scientifically. Vis-à-vis this situation, it may be asked why service organizations should even bother to invest in improved assessment procedures. The answer lies partly in the realm of professional ethics, which makes it incumbent upon a social-welfare organization to use the most honest, systematic, and objective methods of evaluating its work. The other part of the answer lies in the need for the field of social welfare to demonstrate—for the sake of survival—its competence in assessing the value of the product sold to the public.

Counterweighing the social-welfare community's relaxed attitude toward service evaluation is a rising chorus of legislators, spokespeople for taxpayers, and representatives of government at all levels demanding increased accountability from agencies and institutions supported by public funds. This movement has given rise to a veritable deluge of books and journals supporting its ideology and describing new techniques as well as demonstration projects aimed at program evaluation. The actual process of building evaluation into practice, however, has lagged far behind.

A second reason for the profession's failure to employ standardized evaluation procedures is their expense in time and in money. Both are undeniably characteristics of social-scientific evaluation methods, but both time and cost have to be judged in relation to the total investment in services. In the absence of adequate evaluation, there is a great likelihood that services may be quite ineffective and represent a far greater cost to the community than the most extensive scientific inquiry.

There is a third factor blocking or retarding efforts at evaluation. This is the credo, widespread among social-helping practitioners, psychiatrists, clinical psychologists, social workers, educational and vocational counselors, and others, that the scientific procedure is not appropriate to their respective fields. This view may represent an honest, intellectual conviction, defensiveness about a service that contains weak spots, or a combination of the two. Formulating an answer to the cognitive position is well beyond the realm of this manual. On the more pragmatic side, it is possible to point to numerous studies done in recent years in such areas as preschool education, mental retardation, and behavior therapy, and to show how these have contributed to the constructive growth of practice.

Referring back to the question of cost and the time required for evaluation procedures, it must be stressed that both can be reduced by stages as the initial expensive efforts at instrument construction and standardization pave the way for studies, both large and small, that utilize the new products. However, a real change in the use of evaluation research by the helping professions will probably not take place until administrators and practitioners come to accept scientific evaluation as a standard component of practice.

IV. Family and Community Functioning: Some Common Denominators and Differences

The Social Work Curriculum Study of 1959 defined the goals of social work as "the enhancement of social functioning wherever the need for such enhancement is either socially or individually perceived" (Boehm, p. 46). *Social functioning* is a unifying concept by which human behavior can be viewed meaningfully within the context of the environment in regard to such criteria as stability, change over time, normalcy, adequacy, and problemicity. The use of the concept social functioning as against such concepts as "adjustment and adaptation denotes an important shift in social work from the study of properties of given objects to the study of relationships among parts of a system or among disparate systems. This shift parallels the similar change in focus in the biological and social sciences that occurred earlier in the century. Function, according to Blaine Mercer, may be defined as "the processes associated with the structure,[1] or, more specifically, those contributions of a part to the continuity and ordered change of the larger whole to which it belongs" (p. 8). The concept of social functioning has the advantage of being applicable to persons as well as to social systems and of being definable in terms of social roles that are relevant to the many-faceted social-work profession.

The application of the concept social functioning has been confined mainly to the study and treatment of individuals and families. Few efforts have been made to extend the concept to such larger social systems as agency, institution, neighborhood, and community, which are also the concerns of the profession. Such an extension calls for an identification of common denominators inherent in the concept's use in relation to specific subject matter, such as economic functioning, health functioning, and welfare functioning. Since the concern of the present manual covers family and community, the discussion here will be confined to these two systems.

Functioning, as stated above, denotes a process in which the

---

1. "Structure" is defined by Mercer as the arrangements of individuals in relationships defined and controlled by patterns of standards and values, customs, or behavioral norms. Definitions of the concepts of function and functioning are derived from the work of Radcliffe-Brown (pp. 178–187).

action of the parts of a system are viewed in relation to their contribution toward its continuity. Within the context of social work, continuity can be defined more normatively as behavior connected with the goals or values of autonomy, integration,[2] and viability of the system (Warren 1970). *Autonomy* means existence as a separate entity, the maintenance of a measure of independence, control over the component parts of the system, and the existence of a positive image of self, supported by the use of symbols that are characteristic of the system. *Integration* denotes interaction that serves to unify and harmonize the constituent elements of the system and fosters interdependence, which furthers its instrumental and expressive goals. *Viability* can be defined as a capacity to confront problems (Warren 1970, p. 223) and to survive under adverse conditions. Stability as well as a capacity for ordered change are characteristics of viability. Autonomy, integration, and viability are abstract concepts that need translating into measurable indicants that are completely relevant to the purposes of the study.

The social-work focus of this book dictates a welfare concern in the broadest sense, by which is meant a consideration of the material, biological, social, and emotional well-being of the individuals composing the system. Individuals may be said to constitute the major constituent parts of the nuclear family— except for such subsidiary systems as parents and siblings, who may on occasion also receive primary emphasis in family research. In the community, by contrast, individuals represent the beginning link in a chain of systems that vary in size, complexity, length of tenure, and other characteristics. Most students of the family are concerned with such properties of the individual as personality, marital satisfaction, sexuality, so-

---

2.   Warren does not include integration but cites "broad distribution of community decision-making power" as one of the three goals. This value was seen as too narrowly focused for applicability to both community and family systems.

cial roles, power, and childrearing practices. To be sure, interactional analysis deals with the variables of subsystems, but such analysis uses the individual as an immediate referent. The study of the community, on the other hand, might be conducted at levels where individual behavior is only of secondary importance as compared with the collective properties of given entities or systems. For instance, a study of industrialization may deal mainly with changes in production, consumption, employment patterns, and the growth of unions, or research on mobility may concern itself with the social, ethnic, and religious composition of census tracts or neighborhoods.

The study of community functioning from the point of view of the welfare of its citizens represents only one of several research foci, without any assumption that the study of the individual is the ultimate or most significant perspective in community analysis.[3] The choice of focus in this project stems from a theoretical orientation whose immediate goal is service to maximize the well-being of the individual and the family. It is this orientation that guides the selection of criteria for the study of social functioning.

Given the general-systems goal dimensions of autonomy, integration, and viability, we need to determine their significance relative to family and community needs. The welfare and service focus of the endeavor decrees an emphasis on the integrative aspects of the system over autonomy and viability. Since we judge the system's effectiveness chiefly in terms of the well-being of its members, our concern is more with the way these are being served than with the system's ability to act independently and to cope with diverse problems, even though

---

3. Homans argues forcefully "that the general explanatory principles even of sociology are not sociological as functionalists would have them be, but psychological, propositions about the behavior of men, not about the behavior of societies" (pp. 809–818).

these may in the long run affect the integrative goals of the system.

At the family level the integrative-goal function is manifest in the family's performance of tasks such as providing security, love, social and intellectual stimulation, and meeting some instrumental needs. Autonomy is inherent in the family's ability to act as a provider—within the limits of the prevailing norms—and to create a sense of family solidarity. Viability resides in the family's capacity for overcoming social, emotional, and economic crises and meeting economics needs.

At the level of the community the integrative goal covers the provision of services and resources for income, employment, housing, social security, health, social adjustment, acceptance, social and cultural participation, and youth as well as adult socialization. Viability pertains to the social-control function of maintaining order, giving legal and physical protection, and enforcing a degree of conformity with community norms. Autonomy, though important in the realm of policy making, is only indirectly measurable at the level of citizens' behavior in the degree to which community members are able, through political and administrative processes, to determine community policy. Autonomy is also reflected in the degree to which the community is able to meet its citizens' instrumental needs by itself. In short, from the perspective of community members in general, the assessment of community functioning revolves mainly around the integrative and viability aspects of the system, while autonomy either plays a secondary role in the life of the resident or is only measurable through complex systems analysis.

This manual's basic approach to studying the social functioning of both family and community is to assess the way in which the individual and collective needs of the members are being met. The degree to which this does or does not happen becomes a criterion for judging the functioning of the respective systems. The similarity in the philosophy of evaluating family and community, however, does not guarantee a similarity in methodology. The reasons for the differences in methodological approaches stem from the nature of the relationship between the individual and the respective system.

Allowing for some exceptions, the individual and the family interact with one another almost continuously and shape each other's functioning and development. The family as a group is aware of the roles of its members and is informed about their behavior, attitudes, and values. Each family member in turn finds her- or himself responding much of the time to the family as a collectivity. Most individuals find, however, that the community is not an entity with which they interact all the time. The closeness of the relationship between community and individual is conditioned, to be sure, by many factors, such as the size, prestige, and power of the community and the status and length of residence of the individual, but most people find that community membership is not as compelling an association as family membership, and their functioning or that of their family is not so strongly influenced by the city, town, or hamlet in which they live. The community, on its part, is not aware— again allowing for some variation due to size and the influence of the individual—of the resident per se but only of groups of taxpayers, commuters, shoppers, demonstrators, etc.

The nature of the foregoing relationships determines the reciprocal expectations between individuals and the systems to which they belong. Such expectations are extensive between individual family members and the family as a system. Individuals are expected to contribute according to their ability, and the family as a whole is expected to meet many of the basic needs of its members. The reciprocal expectations between individual (or family) and community are much more limited in scope. Community residents must pay taxes, obey the laws and ordinances, and conform, more or less, to local mores. But the residents, in turn, have certain expectations regarding the community's obligations toward them. They generally feel entitled to educational and welfare services, to roads, sewers, public transportation, and other utilities either offered directly or through a concessionaire given the community franchise.

Individuals and families are most likely to judge a community by the services it offers, and that judgment is selected here as a basis for measuring community functioning. Citizens' assessment of services is a relatively universal and unambiguous criterion, set in the very complex and infinitely variable pattern of roles, relationships, and functions that characterizes communities. The relationship of individuals to their families, by contrast, is more direct and immediate, permitting ready investigation into the several dimensions in which individuals and families relate to one another and serve each other. Relationships between individuals and families can be identified and evaluated within a framework of cultural norms and expectations. Individual-community relationships, however, are ill defined, except as they overstep the wide boundaries of the law. Without a clear definition they cannot be assessed very readily relative to existing societal standards or norms. This vagueness is, in fact, largely responsible for the lack of definite standards by which such relationships might be judged.

Family and community functioning also suggest substantially different assessment procedures for the collecting of data. In a study of the family each member becomes a potentially valid informant regarding most aspects of family life, while family life as a whole can be studied readily by means of observation, interviews, tape recordings, questionnaires, and other techniques. In community research, however, the average community member has only limited usefulness as a source of information since he or she has been exposed to just a few aspects of community life, and the study itself is so complex, time consuming, and expensive an endeavor as to be beyond the reach of most investigators. Therefore, the study of family functioning is likely to utilize a variety of data-collection techniques that capture many dimensions of family living, while research on community functioning, in avoiding the danger of becoming bogged down in the complexity of data, is prone to make use of a relatively simple and standardized instrument, tapping the most basic information on residents' degree of satisfaction or dissatisfaction with the community's services and resources.

Before discussing the specific approaches to the study of family and community, their functional interrelationship within a research framework deserves additional comment. Arensberg and Kimball, in an essay on the evaluation of community study, state that "the community offers the most significant focus, the most viable form of human groupings, for direct innovation, for massive and continuous stimulation of cultural change" (p. 691). Whether one accepts the superlative formulation "*most* viable" or simply accepts the proposition that the community is *one* important agent for innovation and cultural change, there would seem to be little doubt that the community constitutes the immediate environment within which individuals and families express themselves socially, culturally, and politically and where change and innovation are registered in a tangible manner. In view of this, the study of family that does not address itself fully to the community in which the family resides omits a research aspect that is essential to a full understanding of its life.

The interrelationship between family and community would seem to be particularly pronounced where social service is the focus of research. Social services of one form or another are probably rendered to all community residents. However, certain segments of any population receive more services than others because of their dependence on community-sponsored programs: families with school-aged children, the unemployed or underemployed, other categories of economically deprived, the sick and the physically handicapped, the maladjusted and the mentally ill, old people without financial means, deprived ethnic minorities, and others. The greater the families' depen-

dence on community resources, the greater the interaction
between these families and the community. The needs of a
population affect the total character of the community, its
goals, political processes, service structure, self-image, etc. The
kind of services, facilities, and resources families get from the
community—or in the community, if it serves merely as a
mediator and referral agent—tends to have an impact upon the
functioning and development of these families.

Students of the community have been inclined to look upon
the system as a function of such population factors as social
class, ethnicity, age groupings, migration patterns, and subur-
banization. Less common are efforts to inquire into the effects
of the community upon its residents. The methodological problems inherent in such investigations are considerable because
they require longitudinal designs that permit a tracing of
community influences on matched populations, settling in one
type of community or another. An alternate possibility is offered by repeated cross-sectional studies, in which efforts are
made to deduce the effects over time of different community
systems on comparable population groups.

Social-welfare research affords a special opportunity to study
the influence of the community on the population by testing
the effects of communitywide measures on the incidence and
prevalence of given community problems. The epidemiological
approach, widely employed in public health, is particularly
suited for such research. Programs to remedy, control, or pre-
vent a given problem are generally administered within a
larger social-service context made up of existing resources,
bureaucratic procedures, attitudes of officials, etc. All of these
are related to the way programs are perceived and utilized by
the population for which they are intended, and they, in turn,
are affected by the programs themselves. Therefore, a study of
the effects of programs and services can be made particularly
meaningful by including in the design a measurement of the
most relevant community variables.

The foregoing considerations have spurred the present effort at developing tools that may help to bring into meaningful juxtaposition certain aspects of community and family systems. The common study concept chosen, as stated earlier, is social functioning, and it was operationalized with reference to the needs, problems, and aspirations of populations. This is a selective focus especially attuned to service planning and operation. The instruments that are presented here, like most tools of social measurement, are instruments "in becoming" rather than finished and final products. Researchers are encouraged to view them as prototypes or models for ongoing endeavors and to make whatever adaptations are required by the goals of their study.

The process of measuring family and community functioning is described in this volume under separate headings following a discussion of the theoretical underpinnings of each approach. We shall begin with family functioning, the more familiar of the two concepts and the one that provides the first span of the complex bridge between individuals and the social environment in which they live.

V. Measuring Family
Functioning

1. Introduction

Service to families is not a new phenomenon in social work, for both the Settlement Movement and the early social-casework school in America were oriented toward the family. In the 1930s the focus in casework began to shift significantly toward the individual, partly as a result of the influence of Freudian psychology but also in response to the mushrooming public-welfare programs, which were assuming responsibility for service to families. This left the professional casework agencies free to treat the psychosocial problems of individuals.

In the 1950s professional social work once again directed its attention toward the family, an interest that was shared by segments of the psychiatric profession.[4]

The emphasis of this new movement was, as it should have been, on diagnosis and treatment. The conceptualization underlying practice, though influenced by the social sciences and particularly sociological theory on the family, remained basically *ad hoc* and underdeveloped. There were few efforts by the social-work community to utilize practice in such a way as to test whatever theoretical propositions had been accepted by the practitioners.

If the practice-related family theory was not well developed, practice-focused measurement was practically nonexistent during the 1950s. Kogan and Shyne, reporting on the development of the Community Service Society Movement Scale (Hunt-Kogan Scale), pointed out that initial efforts were directed toward rating the total case (usually a family) and that "this approach stemmed directly from the family-centered approach of the worker involved in the research program" (Kogan and Shyne). The effort at total case or family measurement was eventually abandoned in favor of measuring individual behavior, because of the difficulties workers experienced in rating groups of individuals and because the change in family composition (in follow-up studies) made it impossible to compare before and after ratings. "Many workers," Kogan and Shyne stated, "also reported that they had to judge change in the individual before they could render the judgment for the family" (p. 15).

The crux of the difficulty encountered by the researchers is contained in the last statement. The failure to carry out family measurement stemmed mainly from the fact that the family was viewed as an aggregate of individuals rather than as a social system. If the family is conceptualized as a mere aggre-

---

4.   For an early, well-articulated position see Ackerman.

gate of persons, a change in family structure, such as the withdrawal or addition of one or more individuals, or role changes pose major problems in repeated measurement. If, on the other hand, the family is defined as a system, the turnover of family members is of secondary importance as long as the group of family members continues to operate as a unit carrying out tasks that meet ongoing individual as well as group needs.

The measurement endeavor reported here is a revised version of the St. Paul Scale, an evaluative method developed in the late 1950s in conjunction with the Family Centered Project of St. Paul, Minnesota (Geismar and Ayres). The Scale was originally devised for evaluating the social functioning of socially disorganized families, but it has more recently been used in slightly revised form in research with normal families as well. Differences in the application of the Scale to one type of population or another will be dealt with following a discussion of the instrument itself.

2. *Theoretical Underpinnings*

In the quest for a universal definition of the family, anthropologists and sociologists have been studying and comparing primitive and technologically advanced societies (Bell and Vogel, pp. 37-47; Christensen, pp. 401-500; Reiss). The extensive variations in structure and function pose problems for the scholar who is intent upon formulating definitions that are true common denominators. Our task of definition is made easier by the fact that our research is confined to families (most English speaking) living in western cultures. In our study the family is structurally a group of two or more people, including at least one parent or parent substitute and one dependent child, related by blood, marriage, or adoption. The group is held together by moral, social, and legal rights and obligations and carries out socially expected functions that include the socialization of children and the provision of love, security, food, clothing, and shelter for all its members.

The _family_ is a system by virtue of the fact that its constituent parts interact and bear a definable relationship to one another. At one level, this system is composed of persons who reside together, talk to one another, express love or hate to each other, join in certain tasks, help or antagonize each other, engage in sexual intercourse, and communicate in other ways. At another level the family is composed of many roles that are socially defined and stand in some complementary relationship to each other. The roles revolve around efforts to carry out functions leading to the attainment of family objectives that have been spelled out in part by society—these are mainly the legal and moral aspects of such goals—and in part by the family itself, with the aid of relatives, friends, and other reference groups.

By and large, the research effort is directed to the study of the nuclear family composed of parents and dependent children. On occasion the unit of study will deal with various types of extended family, perhaps including grandparents, relatives, children of relatives, and other household members not related by blood. Measurement will take account of these individuals to the extent that they may be considered part of the family system, or, put differently, to the extent that their roles mesh with the roles of nuclear-family members.

Following Bell and Vogel (pp. 6–33) and other writers whose names are commonly identified with the structural-functional approach in the study of the family,[5] a guiding proposition of the present study is that an individual family is a social system, with functional requirements or prerequisites comparable to those of other social systems.

---

5. For reviews of the structural-functional approach to the study of the family see Pitts and McIntyre.

There is some variation in the way scholars have defined functional prerequisites of the family. Previously we listed autonomy, integration, and viability as perhaps the most basic goals of any social system. The systems themselves, as indicated earlier, differ with regard to the degree of importance each of these goals assumes for the system's continuity. This difference in emphasis determines how functional prerequisites are identified and defined. Moreover, different scholars have conceptualized the function in dissimilar ways in keeping with their own theoretical approaches to the subject.

William J. Goode lists reproduction, status placement, biological maintenance, socialization, and sexual controls as functions classically assigned to the family (p. 188). Marion Levy identifies role differentiation, allocation of solidarity, economic allocation, political allocation, and allocation of integration and expression as so-called "structural prerequisites" rather than functional prerequisites, because his points of reference are the substructures that carry out the functions (McIntyre, pp. 70-71). Kingsley Davis considers reproduction, placement, maintenance, and socialization as core functions of the family while other functions are viewed as by-products of the primary functions (pp. 394-396). All these schemes assign central importance to the integrative aspects of family life.

The social-welfare focus of the present study suggests an organization of functions relative to relationship patterns in the family (intrafamilial relationships), with persons outside the family (extrafamilal relationships), role behavior of individuals, and instrumental forms of behavior, such as maintaining the home and providing for the economic and health needs of family members. The functions, to be identified in more detail below, reflect interaction patterns, roles, and task performances among members of the family system and between members of that system and other surrounding systems, such as work, school, social peer groups for children and adults, neighbors, health and welfare agencies, and formal organizations for sociability and recreation. The conceptualization and organization of functions are designed as an aid in assessing family behavior according to culturally and professionally prescribed norms and to facilitate programming for intervention, because the categorization denotes a grouping of behavior and situations that have their counterpart in the activities of the potential intervener, particularly the social worker.

The reader may be interested in learning how the scheme for categorizing family functions evolved, and a momentary departure from the discussion of the theoretical framework may be in order. Work on the scheme known as the St. Paul Scale of Family Functioning has been characterized by an interweaving of both the empirical and theoretical. The Scale categories were derived from a social diagnostic study originally developed and used by a group of caseworkers in the Services to Families and Children Project sponsored jointly by the New York City Youth Board and the Department of Welfare. The social diagnostic study was introduced to the Family Centered Project by Alice Overton, Project Director from 1955 to 1959 and formerly coordinator of the New York Project.

The Family Centered Project research team, composed of Beverly Ayres and myself, was charged with the development of an instrument for the assessment of movement in multiproblem families. We held regular meetings with Project workers to examine the adequacy of the diagnostic outline, reviewing first of all the category scheme for comprehensiveness of content and exclusiveness of classification—assuring the same content would be included in only one category. This review was based on existing case data that the social workers were discussing in their weekly in-service training seminars. Secondly, we checked the existing classification scheme for the possible omission of content that was included in the case material. To do this we reviewed other family classification systems as well as family case data collected by other investigators in order to establish what family roles, thought to be of importance for understanding and treating families, were not covered by the original scheme.

A conspicuous example of omission was the category "social activities." Its noninclusion reflected a service orientation best characterized as problem-focused, lacking concern with areas of functioning generally free of serious crises. The practitioners responded positively to the suggestion that social activities be included among the social-study categories, for it reinforced an already present conviction that effective service to families must build upon strengths as well as weaknesses.

These empirically derived categories would have utility for research only if they could be organized in a theory-relevant format and operationalized for purposes of measurement. The structure-function approach to studying the family, as indicated above, furnished some important leads to organizing the data, for it led to the identification of functions relative to the part they played in assuring the continuity of the system, without incorporating the equilibrium model or the teleological overtones of some of the writers of the functionalist school (Whitaker).

If measurement is the goal, the most basic procedure is to define criteria by which family functioning can indeed be measured. It must be emphasized that choosing the criteria is also the most controversial of undertakings, since it forces the researchers to play a nontraditional role—at least nontraditional for the bulk of social researchers—by committing them to a normative evaluation procedure.

"A precondition to an evaluation study," Edward Suchman wrote, "is the presence of some activity whose objectives are assumed to have value. . . ." He goes on to define value "as any aspect of a situation, event, or object that is invested with a preferential interest as being 'good,' 'bad,' 'desirable,' 'undesirable,' or the like" (pp. 32–33). Values are, of course, relevant to social services and to the helping professions. As administrators, professionals, and the public make decisions on the rendering of services, so they also commit themselves, explicitly or implicitly, to the objectives of these services. Since the services are generally rendered to individuals or groups, the definition of objectives must be expressed in terms of characteristics or qualities attached to the objects of service. A listing of such characteristics or qualities in terms of better or worse, more or less desirable, denotes a listing of values.

In designing social-work services to families, goals need to be formulated that bear a relationship to what it is in families that is viewed as good or desirable. People will more readily agree on the fundamentals of the good life, such as happiness, health, and security, than on the specifics under this heading. It is not altogether certain that a broad, common denominator or desiderata can be formulated for any one society, let alone for all of humankind. Nonetheless—and here is where the researcher has to go out on a limb—evaluation study requires a pinning down of factors by which an activity can be judged. The activity around which present evaluation efforts revolve is professional social work. Therefore, the social-work practitioner who defines treatment goals for families should be able to supply the most relevant list of standards of functioning by which the effectiveness of service can be judged.

The foregoing assumption guided the scale-construction activity in the St. Paul Family Centered Project not only in relation to choice of categories of functioning (see above) but also in the selection of criteria for assessing the quality of family functioning. Through a perusal of workers' statements on treatment goals for families and with the aid of a social-worker-researcher dialogue aimed at clarifying service goals that were implied but not enunciated, it was possible to evolve a composite measure for evaluating family functioning. This measure comprises two broad dimensions on which professional judgment is being made. The first we shall call the *health-welfare dimension,* and it concerns the basic total well-being and happiness of family members. The second is the

conformity-deviance dimension, which determines the extent to
which family members as a group, subgroup, or as individuals
are integrated into or are at odds with various social systems,
such as family, community, and society.

The health-welfare dimension, which is rooted in the concept
of human need, takes account of the fact—and treats it as an
assumption in this study—that needs and wants (the most
pressing of needs denoting a deficit in a requirement) are
powerful forces motivating human behavior. The complexity of
the need concept, its variability, and inferential nature (it is
extraordinarily difficult to measure it directly) preclude its use
as a separate variable in our conceptual scheme.[6]

The conformity-deviance discussion builds on the notion that
all viable social systems require a measure of compliance on
the part of those, individual or groups, who make up the system. Without a degree of conformity the system will either not
function or operate at such a low level of effectiveness as to
threaten survival. If compliance may be assumed to represent
one of the system's needs—related to its goals of viability and
integration—conformity must also be viewed as a need of individuals for the reason that in their role of family members they
have much to gain (a sense of belonging, other psychological as
well as material rewards) by falling into line.

The health-welfare dimension includes two subareas that
deal with the following two questions: does behavior contribute
to or is it harmful to the physical, social, and emotional well-
being of family members or to the welfare of the whole family
system or one of its subsystems? and is a family member's
behavior personally satisfying and commensurate with his or

---

6. The concept need was used also in the discussion of community
functioning as an organizing construct for differentiating among two
types of provisions for services: primary provisions assumed to be
related to survival needs and secondary provisions seen to rest on
needs denoting a lesser degree of urgency.

her potential for social functioning? The conformity-deviance dimension also is composed of two subareas that address themselves to the following questions: are laws observed or violated? and is behavior in harmony or in conflict with the mores and standards of a community or a family's status group? These four subdimensions are to be viewed as common denominators of criteria for evaluating functioning, and they need to be specified further in relation to particular categories of behavior. For instance, with regard to the care of children, the health-welfare dimension suggests that children should feel loved, physically and socially secure, be adequately clothed and fed, etc., while the conformity-deviance dimension implies that they should feel accepted by others, that their behavior should not be outside the law or in violation of the norms of their parents and peer groups, and so forth.

On the other hand, it needs to be stated that not all subdimensions are equally applicable to all types of family functioning. For some forms of behavior one kind of subarea is likely to be of far greater importance than the other. For instance, in seeking to determine the adequacy of a marital relationship, the question of whether partners meet each other's emotional, sexual, and social needs (health-welfare dimension) figures much more prominently than the issue of whether their relationship is a legal one or is condoned by the community.

By identifying the dimensions for judging social functioning we have only delineated the direction of evaluation. To complete the process it is also necessary to define the limits of the dimensions that will determine whether functioning is held to be good or bad, desirable or undesirable. The definition of limits, like the identification of the dimensions, was accomplished by reviewing the treatment plans of social workers and their decisions to close cases because treatment goals were deemed to have been attained. Additionally, however, the researchers found it necessary to review both the casework literature and family- and child-welfare legislation in order to determine cut-off points of adequacy-inadequacy. These boundaries were, in fact, a combination of legal and professional considerations. The former pertain mainly to behavior officially stamped undesirable by the community or its delegated representative and generally declared as a reason for intervention. The latter concern professional judgment on what is and what is not desirable, especially in areas where the law or local statutes do not specify the limits of the allowable.

By and large, law and professional judgment supplement each other. The limits of the law in the area of family and child welfare are wide and leave much undefined territory. Professional judgment seeks to operate within the limits of the law and to provide guidance in areas of behavior where the law supplies none. Occasions arise, nonetheless, when the law and professional standards are in conflict. This occurs most commonly with regard to archaic, or sometimes plainly unenlightened, legislation in the area of conjugal relations, birth control, and the rights of low-income tenants. In those instances, the decision on cut-off points for rating family functioning was guided by professional rather than legal standards.

Before presenting the criteria for rating family functioning, the product of a one-year research effort, it may be helpful to tie together in tabular form the chain of conceptual formulations leading to an evaluation of family functioning.

Chart 1 shows the functional prerequisites of the family organized in terms of nine areas of social functioning. As was pointed out previously, this special form of categorization was found suitable for relating family data to programs of social intervention. The category Relationship to Intervention Worker, in particular, is relevant to this focus of study and should be omitted where programs of services are not involved. The predominant frame of reference for the organization of categories are lower-class families. For that reason no attempt

Chart 1 CONCEPTUAL FRAMEWORK FOR RATING FAMILY FUNCTIONING

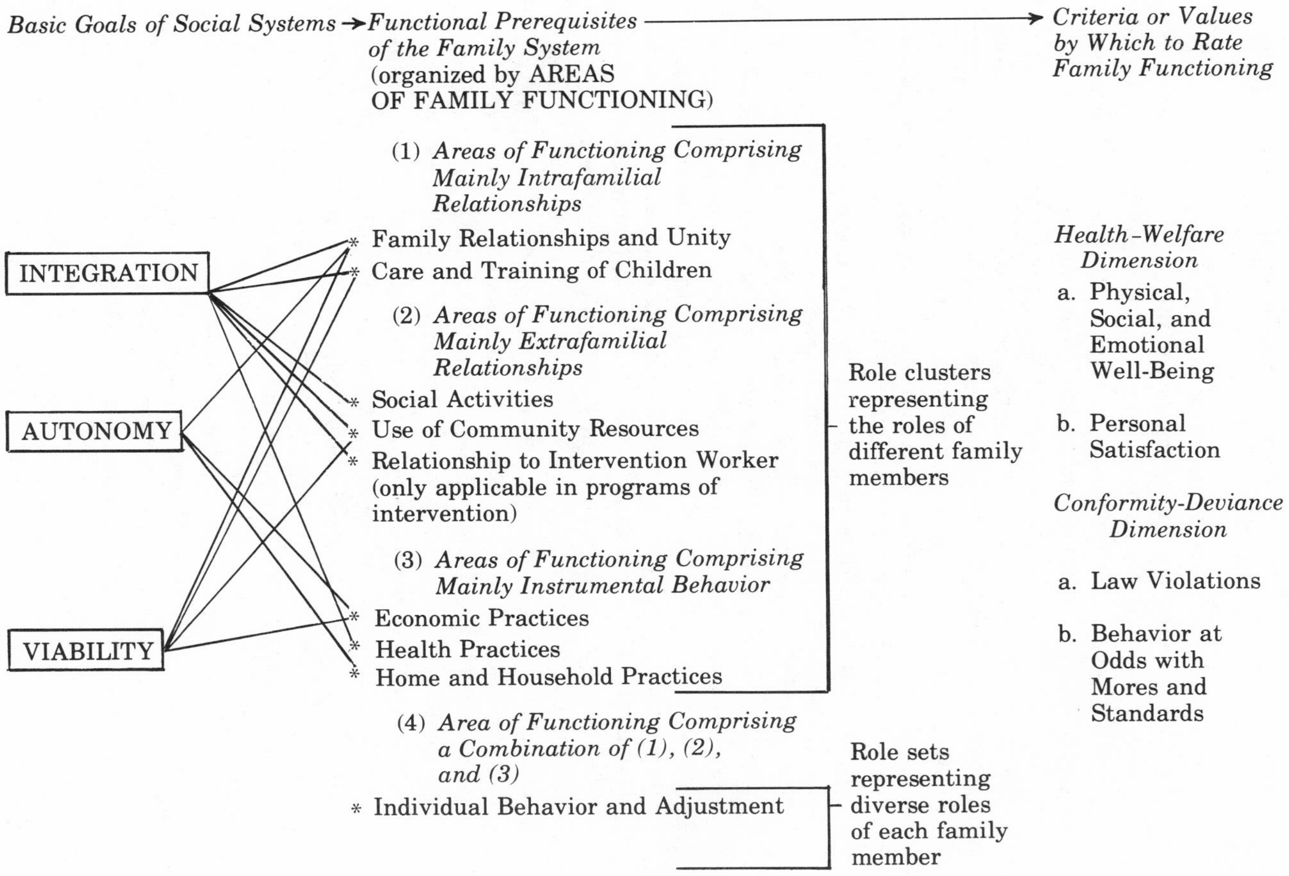

Basic Goals of Social Systems → Functional Prerequisites of the Family System (organized by AREAS OF FAMILY FUNCTIONING) → Criteria or Values by Which to Rate Family Functioning

INTEGRATION

AUTONOMY

VIABILITY

(1) *Areas of Functioning Comprising Mainly Intrafamilial Relationships*

Family Relationships and Unity
Care and Training of Children

(2) *Areas of Functioning Comprising Mainly Extrafamilial Relationships*

Social Activities
Use of Community Resources
Relationship to Intervention Worker (only applicable in programs of intervention)

(3) *Areas of Functioning Comprising Mainly Instrumental Behavior*

Economic Practices
Health Practices
Home and Household Practices

(4) *Area of Functioning Comprising a Combination of (1), (2), and (3)*

* Individual Behavior and Adjustment

Role clusters representing the roles of different family members

Role sets representing diverse roles of each family member

Health–Welfare Dimension

a. Physical, Social, and Emotional Well-Being

b. Personal Satisfaction

Conformity–Deviance Dimension

a. Law Violations

b. Behavior at Odds with Mores and Standards

was made to detail political functioning, for instance, generally viewed as being characteristic of the upper middle class or of elite groups among the lower classes. Political functioning in our scheme is subsumed under the area Social Activities in general and the subarea of Formal Associations.

Religious functioning is another example of a type of family behavior not given separate coverage. Religious functioning is much more limited in scope among urban lower- or working-class families than among the rural population or the urban middle class. Religious functioning in the above scheme is covering under the areas Social Activities (subcategory Formal Associations) and Use of Community Resources (subcategory Religious Institutions). Any measurement undertaken with families in which political or religious functioning plays a prominent role should make provisions for a separate assessment of these two types of functioning.

An important conceptual distinction is to be noted among the nine areas of family functioning shown in Chart 1. Eight of these, all but Individual Behavior and Adjustment, denote areas of functioning where individual roles converge and cluster in order to accomplish given tasks, such as rearing children or keeping house. Individual Behavior and Adjustment, by contrast, signifies role sets of individuals defined as "the complex of positions in which an individual holds simultaneous membership" (Thomas and Biddle, p. 47). It follows that an evaluation of Individual Behavior and Adjustment takes into account the way an individual functions in her or his diverse, socially assigned roles. The adult female in a family, for example, would be rated by the way she performs her roles as wife, mother, homemaker, neighbor, member of the P.T.A., etc. Her male child would be judged in terms of his performance as son, student, peer group member, newspaper boy, and others.

In rating the areas of functioning that represent clusters of the roles of individual family members, our chief concern is not with the individuals themselves but with the way in which the tasks or functions are carried out. In other words, in rating Economic Practices we are interested in the way the functions of providing an income and managing the money are performed. The functionaries, i.e., those who earn the money and budget it, are of secondary importance. In assessing Individual Behavior and Adjustment, on the other hand, individuals or functionaries need to be rated, and that rating is based on the way they manage their role set or perform the various roles assigned to them. Chart 2 provides a simplified example of the relationship between social roles and individual behavior and functions.

The next two sections, numbers 3 and 4, will detail the procedure for collecting and presenting data on family functioning in an organized form. Section 5 gives a listing of criteria for rating the content in each area and subarea. Subsequent steps comprise instructions for rating the families' social functioning and for statistical analysis. A case study of a family is used to illustrate the rating process in a more tangible fashion.

3. Documenting the Families' Social Functioning

The decision to gather information with the aid of an open-ended schedule followed experimentation with a more structured tool, the multiple-choice questionnaire. The open-ended or semi-structured schedule was eventually decided upon for several reasons. It is usable both as an interview schedule in the questioning of respondents and as a schedule for ordering available data such as are found in agency case records, psychiatric protocols, diaries, etc. It permits the bringing together of information from multiple sources. It also makes possible the collection of pertinent data from heterogeneous samples of families. The latter point is important when the specific nature of the families to be studied is not yet known.

Chart 2   RELATIONSHIP BETWEEN SOCIAL ROLES, INDIVIDUAL BEHAVIOR, AND FUNCTIONS

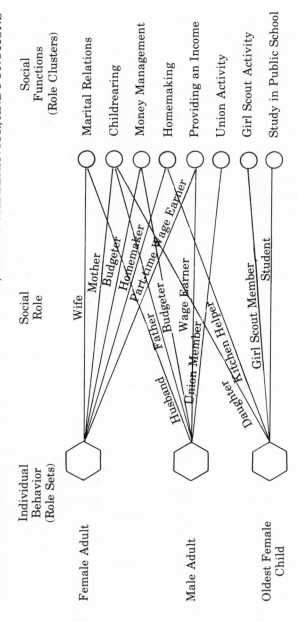

Individual Behavior (Role Sets)	Social Role	Social Functions (Role Clusters)

Female Adult

Male Adult

Oldest Female Child

Wife · Mother · Budgeter · Homemaker · Part-time Wage Earner · Husband · Father · Budgeter · Wage Earner · Union Member · Daughter · Kitchen Helper · Girl Scout Member · Student

Marital Relations · Childrearing · Money Management · Homemaking · Providing an Income · Union Activity · Girl Scout Activity · Study in Public School

When structured instruments are constructed, on the other hand, it is presupposed that prior research has determined the precise universe of content to be collected. That means, in effect, that different structured instruments might be needed if the samples vary in structure or function, or a single comprehensive instrument would be required, one that anticipates all response possibilities—a product that is bound to be lengthy. There is additional advantage to the open-ended schedule. It can be used in an informal interviewer-respondent exchange, which maximizes the chances of motivating the respondent to volunteer information.

Contraposed to the advantages of the open-ended schedule are some disadvantages, as every experienced researcher knows. The data-collection process is harder to standardize. Coding is more difficult. Some of the controls that can be applied in the gathering of prestructured data are missing. Nevertheless, the problems inherent in constructing one bulky, comprehensive questionnaire or smaller, separate forms for each new study are greater than the difficulties presented by the semistructured schedule. Perhaps the major prerequisite for its successful use is the availability of skilled and well-trained interviewers. Because the items in the schedule are more general than questionnaire items, they require translating into a more specific format. For instance, "social outlets of family members" under the area heading Social Activities and subheading Informal Associations needs to supply the answers to such questions as the following: What do family members do for sociability? How do they enjoy themselves? What informal groups do they belong to? How long do the associations last? It follows that interviewers using the open-ended schedule have to understand very clearly the meaning of abstract formulations about family functioning, so that they may be able to translate them into the meaningful and relevant items called for in each situation.

If the open-ended schedule is used it is necessary to have the interview conducted in a relaxed and informal atmosphere where the respondent can answer freely. The interviewer can encourage freedom of expression by letting the respondent move from subject to subject in a manner he or she considers most meaningful. Notes may be taken inconspicuously or the interview may be taped (with permission of the respondent) in order to minimize interference with the flow of information. Thorough knowledge of the schedule will enable the interviewer to request—unobtrusively—items of information not yet covered without breaking the continuity of the exchange. It is also possible to divide interviews into several sessions, thereby reducing respondent fatigue. It has been our experience that the skillfully conducted interview generally represents a pleasant experience for the interviewee; there have been very few break-offs once the respondent has been engaged in discussion.

We have found that it is necessary for interviewers using the schedule on Family Functioning to have had prior experience in handling family data in a conceptual manner. Furthermore, trial interviews should be carried out, in which the interviewer can demonstrate the ability to motivate the respondent and to guide her or him in supplying the relevant material. If available information is used, the data collector must be able to select appropriate content from that which is given. The kind of unstructured interviewing this schedule demands leaves more room for the injection of interviewer bias than does structured interviewing, and the interviewer needs a fair measure of sophistication to guard against this.

The narrative account of a family's social functioning, organized by areas and subareas, will be referred to as the Profile of Family Functioning. The outline used for writing the Profile, tested through the study of hundreds of families, has been found to be a reasonably comprehensive instrument able to gather information about the average family whether young or old, rich or poor, stable or disorganized. At the same time, we must concede that this outline is general and may need to be modified for the study of specific populations or problems. We have on various occasions set up modified forms covering one area or another, as the need arises. For example, it was found that a substitute schedule for the subarea Marital Relationship is helpful in research with out-of-wedlock mothers. Likewise, in the study of families with children in institutions, a special schedule for Individual Behavior and Adjustment/Children Placed was required. That schedule included special items dealing with the child's experience in the institution and with various psychological dimensions of child development, which constituted an important aspect of that particular study.

The interviewer or collector of data from available information will rarely find information on every single item listed in the schedule. Where seemingly essential items are not known, it should be noted in the narrative according to instructions given below. The coder of the Profile of Family Functioning will have to decide whether or not there is sufficient information to code a particular category. On the other hand, the Profile writer may wish to collect relevant information beyond that requested in the outline. There is always room for such, especially since the writer makes no claim for completeness. A substantial extension of data collection that is clearly over and above the requirements of the schedule had best be done with the aid of a revised form, the content of which is dictated by the needs of the study.

The first two areas in the outline contain a subsection called "History." Under A. *Family Relationships and Family Unity,* the collection of historic information applies only to the Marital Relationship, while under B. *Individual Behavior and Adjustment,* history refers to the functioning of each family member except a newborn. The historic data supply background knowledge for rating present functioning, but they are not rated by themselves. There is no way to determine exactly how extensive the information on the background of marriage and individual behavior needs to be in order to make rating of present functioning most meaningful. Some information, it would seem, it indispensable in order to code present behavior within a broader context of cultural norms and expectations, but complete data on every item under family history should be regarded as optional.

By far the most important set of instructions for profiling family functioning pertains to the nature of reporting. The Profile calls essentially for descriptive information on all aspects covered by the categories and subcategories. Evaluative statements or diagnostic terminology is to be avoided except as it can be documented by a description of the actual behavior or situation or by the results of objective assessments in the form of tests, examinations, school grades, and the like. Members of the helping professions, such as social work, clinical psychology, and psychiatry, who are prone to assemble diagnostic material that is problem-focused, may need to be reminded that when writing the Profile of Family Functioning comparable emphasis must be given to the strengths as well as the weaknesses in family life.

A question frequently asked is whether, in instances where the collection of family-functioning data is tied to a service project, research information should be collected by the person rendering the services. This writer observed that most researchers almost instinctively tend to respond to this suggestion in a negative manner. The danger of lack of objectivity on the part of a worker who is professionally involved with or committed to a respondent is usually cited. There is little doubt that the dangers of mixing and possibly confusing the roles of researcher and practitioner are real. Therefore, we would tend to adhere to the general rule of thumb calling for role separation and the employment of interviewers to work independently from the service practitioner.

There is, nonetheless, another consideration that must enter a decision on this matter. If the interviewing is to be effective it is highly desirable that a positive relationship exist between interviewer and respondent. The entry of a research interviewer into a situation where a treatment worker has already been gathering comparable information may constitute a demand that the respondent resents or rejects. The response may range all the way from outright refusal to a more subtle withholding of full cooperation. The latter could take the form of not giving all the information the interviewer is seeking or of giving biased information, and this need not be deliberate but may take a subconscious form.

When making a decision on who will gather the research data, the risk of getting biased data must be weighed against the other, and sometimes greater, risk of obtaining superficial or incomplete data, which may be biased as well. A solution to this dilemma may take several forms. The research project and the service worker may make special efforts from the beginning of treatment to prepare the respondent, who is also a client, for the entry of the research interviewer, and special incentives in the form of monetary rewards or the sharing of research information may be provided to maximize the chances for client collaboration. An alternative to this arrangement, to be employed when it is impossible to separate research interviewers for all cases, is to set up special controls to reduce bias in the data collection of practitioners. These may include a tighter structuring of the research schedule, additional training for practitioners in research interviewing, and the application of quality-control techniques by comparing—through duplicate interviewing—the data collected by practitioners with those gathered by a research interviewer on every Nth case in the study.

4.   *Outline for Preparing a Profile of Family Functioning*

General Instructions: The information to be gathered under the outline headings should be written on sheets of paper that are blank except for a listing of the capitalized headings (areas of family functioning preceded by a capital letter) and under-lined headings (subareas preceded by numerals, also history and present functioning). Three pages each should be re-served for areas *A* (Family Relationships and Family Unity) and *B* (Individual Behavior and Adjustment), while one page will suffice for each of the remaining areas or main categories.

One Profile constitutes a cross-sectional picture of family functioning, i.e., a documentation of social functioning during a limited time span. The first Profile also includes historical information on the marriage and on the individual behavior of family members, which need not be repeated in the second and—if applicable—subsequent Profiles. However, the Profiles following the first should report under each heading develop-ments that have occurred since the writing of the previous Profile. If there have been no changes whatsoever since the previous write-up, this also should be noted.

Seek to cover every item of information, particularly in rela-tion to the family's present functioning. Whenever it is found that an item is not applicable—such as Relationship Among Children when there is but one child—note this by using the initials N.A. (not applicable). Whenever you are unable to provide information because the interviewer failed to obtain it or because it was not found in the available data, use the initials N.K., indicating that the information is not known.

Data collection under area *H. Relationship to Social Worker,* or to another professional practitioner carrying out social intervention, is only appropriate if a special intervention program was taking place at the time of the study or if the family in question was being studied by the agency rendering treatment services. Where this is not the case but families happen to be receiving psychotherapy or another form of help-ing service, that fact can be recorded under *B. Individual Behavior and Adjustment* and *I. Use of Community Resources.*

The need for descriptive, nonevaluative reporting in Profile writing cannot be stressed too heavily. Where evaluative statements are used, they must be backed up by examples of the behavior or functioning leading to the use of these concepts. Diagnostic terminology should be employed only when supported by test scores, results of examinations, or expert judgment. The outline itself follows below.

OUTLINE FOR PROFILING FAMILY FUNCTIONING

A. FAMILY RELATIONSHIPS AND FAMIILY UNITY

1. *Marital Relationship*

a. *History*

Circumstances leading to marriage or consensual union: how did you meet? when? where? was there a formal engagement? what made you decide to get married or live together? how did both sets of parents feel about the union? when were you married? where? who performed the ceremony?

Postmarital adjustment, first years: where did you live? how far from husband's or wife's parents? how often did you exchange visits? how did you get along with parents and in-laws? job situation; financial resources; emotional and social adjustment; sexual adjustment and relative importance of sex in married life; use of birth control; how many children do (did) you desire? how would you prefer (have preferred) to space them?

Early image of marriage: agreement or discrepancy between image before marriage and actual experience; degree of realism of premarital image; knowledge of sex before marriage; source of such knowledge; premarital sex experience.

Arrival of first child: planned vs. unplanned pregnancy;
   physical and emotional health of mother during pregnancy; husband's and wife's attitudes toward child during pregnancy and after his (her) arrival.

b. *Present Functioning*

Degree of love and compatibility: how well do the partners
   get along generally? agreement or disagreement in
   tastes, interests, views, temperaments.

Closeness of emotional ties vs. estrangement and conflict:
   what kind of emotional relationship? what does wife
   expect and what does she get regarding tenderness,
   demonstrated affection, considerateness of feelings,
   moods, irritations, temper? same for husband—what
   does he expect of wife? what does he get?

Interdependence and independence between partners; degree of sharing; talking out feelings; agreements and
   disagreements, both regarding marriage and outside affairs.

Sources of satisfaction and dissatisfaction: inside and outside
   marriage, as regards friends, relatives, job, social and
   cultural pursuits; family goals: what do spouses want on
   a long-term basis?

Agreements and disagreements: their sources; who makes
   decisions? about what? what are the results? is there a
   division of labor? what is its nature and how satisfactory
   is it? any other differences, disagreements, or problems?
   how are they handled?

Sexual adjustment: frequency of sex relations; how important and how satisfying to each?

Responsibility for financial support: who bears it? how well
   is it met?

Extramarital relationships: how long in progress? how casual or intensive? is marriage partner aware of it and how has he or she reacted?

Mutual role expectations: what does the wife see as her husband's and her own duties and responsibilities? how does the husband see this? do their views agree or differ? what are the effects?

Part played by separated partners: if couple is separated, give detailed description of present relationship; extent to which legal obligations are met.

2. *Relationship Between Parents and Children*

Degree of affection between children and parents.

Display vs. concealment of emotions: how are they displayed—holding and cuddling, playing, etc.? amount of care and helping done by the husband, if any; how satisfying is arrangement for care and discipline to each partner?

Degree of respect of children for parents.

Parents' respect for children's rights; how much understanding does each parent have of infantile behavior, i.e., the demands and needs of young children, especially when it interferes with parents' comfort and freedom? do parents understand the needs of older children?

Indifference or rejection.

Favoritism shown by parents.

Companionship and shared activities: what kind of activities does each parent share with the children?

3. *Relationship Among Children*

Degree of closeness, loyalty, affection among children.

Pride in siblings' achievements.

Playing patterns, sharing of possessions.

Cooperation vs. resentment.

Areas of agreement and conflict: fighting, teasing, bullying.

4. *Family Solidarity*

Sense of family identity: cohesiveness vs. individual solitude and isolation of family members; do the members of the family generally "go it together" or is there a pattern of going separate ways?

Reciprocal values, goals, and expectations: values shared vs. values that divide the family.

Family traditions and ritual, shared customs: what, if any, are family traditions? this might include what may have been adopted from their own parents and is still shared with them.

Degree of affection and emotional warmth vs. conflict and indifference among family members.

Pride in family, pulling together in times of stress.

Shared activities: meals, recreation, travel; planning for common goals.

Nature of decision-making process: is it individual or group?

The use of cultural media, such as movies, T.V., radio, books, magazines, etc., as part of family life.

5. *Relationship with Other Household Members*

Nature of relationships with household members (specify who they are) who are not part of the nuclear family.

Degree to which other household members share in or are excluded from family life.

Benefits and problems inherent in a combined living arrangement: who benefits and who is harmed? in what manner? effect of arrangement on family's economic situation, sense of identity.

B. INDIVIDUAL BEHAVIOR AND ADJUSTMENT

Under separate headings cover the behavior and adjustment of 1. Father, 2. Mother, 3. Oldest child at home, 4. Second oldest child, 5. Third oldest child, etc. For each individual list birthdates after first name and date(s) of marriage where applicable. Divide the narrative on each family member into two parts: 1. history, and 2. present functioning.

1. *History*

Structure of family of orientation; nativity of parents; religion of parents; amount of education of parents; size of family; one or both parents in the home; number of siblings; ordinal position of respondent; out-of-wedlock children.

Social and emotional atmosphere of parental home; affection and solidarity vs. conflict; marital relationship of parents; relationship to parents; sibling relationships; health of parents; separations or other crises in family; basic values of the home (religious, ethical, levels of aspiration).

Socioeconomic status of parental home: occupation and income; regularity of income; work patterns; type of residence (rural-urban); characteristics of neighborhood; pattern of social activities.

Education, training, and job experience of husband and wife prior to marriage; type of schools attended; reasons for leaving school; occupational training; jobs held before marriage; talents and hobbies.

Social adjustment before present marriage; type of adjustment at home and after leaving home (if applicable);
social, emotional, and health problems; delinquency and
other deviant behavior; social activities and leisure; patterns of dating; social status of siblings.

2. *Present Functioning*

a. *Factors to be considered for PARENTS* (family of
procreation):

General characteristics: appearance, mannerisms, personality traits, ideas, values, attitudes, interests, education,
and intelligence levels. Give brief physical description of
each parent.

Social behavior: adaptive behavior, social skills, relationships with people and institutions; social conformity vs.
deviance; handicapping traits and attitudes; law
violations; drinking, drug addiction, deviant sexual behavior; other forms of deviant behavior.

Mental-physical state: personality structure, mental health,
emotional disorder, internal conflict, mental retardation, chronic and/or serious disease.

Role performance: as spouse, breadwinner, homemaker,
neighbor, member of the community, participant in
trade and professional associations, member of clubs,
lodges, special programs, etc.; nature and degree of role
involvement; acceptance vs. rejection by role partners;
personal competence for role playing; degree of satisfaction derived. Draw on agency records, psychiatric evaluations, police and probation records, as well as your own
observations.

b. *Factors to be considered for CHILDREN:*

General characteristics: same as for parents.

Social behavior: same as for parents.

Mental-physical state: same as for parents.

Role performance: as child in home setting, sibling, pupil, member of peer groups, play groups, etc.; nature and degree of role involvement; acceptance vs. rejection by role partners; personal competence for role playing; degree of satisfaction derived. Draw on school and camp reports, psychiatric and psychological summaries, test results, police and probation records, as well as your own observations.

C. CARE AND TRAINING OF CHILDREN

1. *Physical Care*

Physical appearance.

Supply and condition of clothing.

Nutrition.

Attention given to cleanliness, diet, and health needs.

In the case of infants, give the schedule of the mother's care.

2. *Training Methods and Emotional Care*

Affection, indifference, rejection, rigidity, overpermissiveness.

Kind of punishment used (or contemplated in the case of an infant): appropriateness of discipline to behavior; discipline by whom, for what? consistency of discipline, family rules; agreement between parents over exercise of discipline; approval of good conduct (whether given).

Encouragement of independence vs. fostering of dependence.

Differential treatment of siblings.

Behavior standards set by parents.

D. SOCIAL ACTIVITIES

1. *Informal Associations*

Relationships with parents, in-laws, friends and neighbors: their nature and frequency.

Social outlets of family members.

Antisocial acts; their nature and motivation.

Identification with larger groups, i.e., neighborhood, community.

Socialization experience for children beyond the nuclear family.

Ways in which free time is spent informally.

2. *Formal Associations*

Membership of family members in organized groups (social, economic, political, and recreational).

Attitude toward organized groups and activities (include unions, lodges, religious groups, etc.).

Type of activity in groups: nominal memberships vs. leadership or committee memberships.

Degree of satisfaction derived from formal associations.

E. ECONOMIC PRACTICES

1. *Source(s) and Amount of Family Income*

Employment, public assistance, insurance, support from relatives.

Adequacy of income relative to family's needs.

Satisfaction with income.

Necessities provided?

2. *Job Situation* (applies to family members who contribute substantially to support of family)

Nature of work, employment practices.

Behavior on job, attitude toward employment.

Relations with boss and co-workers.

Satisfaction or dissatisfaction with job.

Suitability of job for person's capabilities.

Frequency of job changes.

Reaction of spouse and children to job situation.

3. *Use of Money*

Ability to manage money: who manages the money? who decides on expenditures? agreement vs. disagreement over money management.

Budgeting: haphazard or systematic? use of banks, methods of saving, insurances.

Priorities for spending money: realistic regard to basic necessities?

Amount and nature of debts, reason for debts.

F. HOME AND HOUSEHOLD PRACTICES

1. *Physical Facilities*

Type of home, age, ownership (public, private), number of rooms, arrangement of rooms, privacy, crowding.

Physical condition of home.

Characteristics of neighborhood: types of buildings and their age; conditions of buildings and yards; nature of street scene: traffic, people on the streets, cleanliness, etc.

Adequacy of basic household equipment: furnishings for sleeping, bathing, refrigeration, cooking, sanitation, recreation.

Attitude toward home: attention to making it attractive vs. neglect.

2. *Housekeeping Standards*

Management of household chores: how assigned, executed?

Ways of serving meals and adequacy of diet; timing and regularity of meals.

Buying patterns: food, clothing, recreation, car, furniture, etc.

Neatness of home: pride vs. indifference regarding management of the household.

G. HEALTH CONDITIONS AND PRACTICES

1. *Health Conditions* (include a paragraph on each family member)

Health of family members: adequate, normal functioning? problems, diseases, handicaps, debilitating conditions, mental illness?

2. *Health Practices*

Medical care obtained or avoided?

Use of preventive resources: well-baby clinic, immunization, medical check-ups.

Care exercised in following medical instructions?

Disease-prevention practices; physical-hygiene practices.

Dental care: regularity, hygiene.

H. RELATIONSHIP TO SOCIAL OR OTHER INTERVENTION WORKER (see general instructions, above)

1. *Attitude Toward Worker*

Opinions expressed by client family; attitudes reflected in their behavior; is family cooperative, indifferent, hostile, suspicious, etc.? which family members reveal what kinds of attitudes toward professional intervention?

2. *Use of Worker*

Manner in which client uses worker: for advice, guidance, concrete help, dealing with problems, venting feelings, manipulation, etc. what does client expect from worker?

I. USE OF COMMUNITY RESOURCES

1. *School* (include primary, secondary, and adult education)

Value parents place on education, their attitudes toward the school.

Interest they take in children's school activities, contact with school personnel.

Children's attitudes toward school, achievement, attendance, behavior.

2. *Religious Institutions* (Church or Synagogue) (check "not appropriate" if no contact or nominal tie only)

Membership and attendance; denomination.

Type of participation: services, religious school, church clubs and activities, etc.

Satisfaction derived from attendance.

Agreement of parents on children's participation.

Influence of church or synagogue membership on family solidarity.

3. *Health Resources* (include only physical health)

Type of services used: public; private; clinics; out-patient departments; etc.
Knowledge about and attitude toward resources: cooperative; apathetic; suspicious; hostile; resentful; etc.

Use of agencies: appointments kept or missed; medical advice used or disregarded.

4. *Social Agencies* (include penal and correctional services, such as Probation and Parole, Housing Authorities, employment agencies, Public Welfare, family-planning services, social-adjustment services—general and sectarian, mental health and hygiene clinics, etc.)

Knowledge about and attitude toward agencies; well or poorly informed; favorable attitudes; hostile; resentful; apathetic; defensive; etc.

Use of agencies: source of referral; family seeks help; is cooperative; uses agency appropriately; overly demanding; refuses to accept agency services; etc.

5. *Recreational Agencies* (include clubs, community and neighborhood centers, organized playgrounds, public and private recreation programs and services, recreation camps, etc.)

Knowledge and use made of recreational agencies by children; frequency and regularity of use.

Parents' use of and attitude toward recreational facilities for children and adults.

Additional Instructions for Profile Writing

(1) The first step to be taken when writing a Profile of Family Functioning is to review thoroughly all areas or main categories and subcategories. This will enable the writer, whether interviewer or arranger of available data, to organize the information in a manner that fits the Profile structure. An interviewer who has already conducted the interview and has thus become acquainted with the schedule will have to rearrange her or his handwritten notes or the tape-recorded transcript. If the information is being taken from available data, some time will be needed to reorganize them to fit the Profile format.

(2) The first Profile, which covers information gathered at the start of the study, should be written with a clear terminal date in mind. Information beyond that date belongs to the second Profile, or to subsequent ones. Conversely, interview material secured in second, third, or later interviews may be found to belong under the beginning situation covered in the first Profile, even though it was not picked up in the initial interview. Room should, therefore, be left in the first Profile for appropriate additions.

(3) Cross-referencing of information helps avoid repetition. Areas and subareas are organized to minimize duplication, but some overlapping is unavoidable. For instance, the physical dis-

ability of the father, the main wage earner, deserves mention under Individual Behavior and Adjustment, Health Conditions and Practices, and Economic Practices. Other areas, such as Family Relationships and Unity and Social Activities, may be affected. A detailed description of the condition, however, need not be given under more than one heading and can be cross-referenced under the others.

(4) The first Profile is the most truly cross-sectional in nature, for it covers the beginning situation, which can be defined as the social functioning of a family during a given time span—let us say a three- or four-week period—preceding the first interview. For certain kinds of officially recorded behavior, such as institutionalizations, incarcerations, or court convictions, it seems appropriate to include in the first Profile information covering the past year. Subsequent Profiles are cross-sectional, with a latitude covering the time span from the previous Profile. Ideally, the time span should not exceed six months, since the accumulation of data for a longer period of time makes rating more difficult. Within the limited time span the Profile is, therefore, a "moving picture" rather than a "snapshot." Thus, if at the time of interviewing a child is behaving normally but has been in trouble frequently during previous months, the "snapshot" type of reporting would give a skewed picture, whereas a description of the longer trend of behavior would give a truer picture of the child's functioning.

5. Rating Family Functioning

A well-written Profile is the prerequisite for an effective evaluation of a family's social functioning. The next step in the evaluative process is the rating of the case narrative, but rating is possible only after the criteria by which the rating or coding is to be done are spelled out.

Chart 1 listed four criteria under the health-welfare and conformity-deviance dimensions that are the composite measure for coding family functioning. The criteria and their respective theoretical dimensions as stated earlier, are not equally applicable to each category of family functioning for the simple reason that criteria of health and welfare and conformity-deviance are not of equal significance in every type of behavior, role playing, or task performance. The issue of conformity-deviance, for example, is likely to figure prominently in a child's student role but is of very minor importance in the planning and serving of meals. Regarding the latter, the question of nutritional balance (health dimension) is, of course, the major issue guiding the ratings on social functioning.

The criteria for evaluating social functioning are formulated at a fairly high level of abstraction. This makes them applicable to a variety of situations but also demands skillful deductive reasoning when coding case material. To facilitate the evaluation process the more generalized or abstract criteria were broken down into more specific types of functioning illustrative of positive versus negative well-being or deviant versus conforming behavior in each area and subcategory of family functioning.

In line with the overall purposes of evaluation, criteria for coding social functioning need to be laid out on an evaluative continuum, ranging from the most positive to the most negative or the most favorable to the most unfavorable, depending on whichever concepts are appropriate to the study. The researchers in the St. Paul Family Centered Project decided to select the designation adequate/inadequate to denote the extremes of the continuum for measurement.

Adequate functioning denotes behavior and situations most conducive to the welfare of the family and its members, while inadequate functioning signifies the opposite. Inadequate functioning is seen as so damaging to the family and/or society as to entitle the community to intervene. Adequate functioning, by contrast, is seen to be in line with community expectations. Adequate and inadequate functioning represent the extreme positions on a seven-point continuum whose midpoint or anchor position is marginal functioning, defined as behavior and situations that are potentially problematic but not sufficiently harmful to justify community intervention on legal grounds. The in-between positions—near adequate, above marginal, below marginal, and near inadequate—represent levels of functioning slightly higher or lower than the others that are spelled out in the criteria for rating functioning. The general criteria for rating family functioning are given below and are followed by a listing of specific criteria by area and subarea.

5a.   Criteria for Rating Family Functioning[7]

I.   General Criteria

INADEQUATE	MARGINAL	ADEQUATE
Functioning Harmful to the Point Where Community Has a Right to Intervene.	Functioning Not Sufficiently Harmful to Justify Intervention.	Functioning is in Line with Community Expectations.
Laws and/or mores are clearly violated. Behavior of family members is a threat to the community.	Major laws are not being violated, although behavior of family members is at variance with status-group expectations.	Laws are obeyed and mores are observed. Behavior is in line with status-group expectations.

7.   Reproduced with permission of the publisher from L. L. Geismar and Beverly Ayres, *Measuring Family Functioning*. St. Paul, Minn.: Family Centered Project, Greater St. Paul Community Chest and Councils, Inc., 1960, pp. 91–100. Some revisions have been made by the Neighborhood Improvement Project, New Haven, Conn., the Rutgers Family Life Improvement Project, Newark, N.J., and later endeavors.

Family life is charac- | Family life is generally | Family members are
terized by extreme con- | marked by conflict, | generally satisfied with
flict, neglect, severe | apathy, or unstable re- | their lot, and their
deprivation, unhappi- | lationships that can be | needs are being met. Ef-
ness, or very poor rela- | seen as a potential | forts aimed at improve-
tionships resulting in | threat to the family's | ment are made where
physical and/or emo- | and/or the community's | appropriate. Family life
tional suffering of fam- | welfare. Family is | is stable; members have
ily members; disruption | poorly equipped to deal | a sense of belonging and
of family life is immi- | with problems; family | sharing mutually com-
nent; children are in | members are frequently | patible goals and expec-
clear and present | dissatisfied with their | tations. Problems are
danger because of above | condition and do not | faced and dealt with ap-
conditions or other be- | possess the knowledge | propriately. Children
havior inimical to their | or ability to improve it. | are being raised in an
welfare. | Although children are | atmosphere conducive
 | not being properly so- | to healthy growth and
 | cialized and their envi- | development. Socializa-
 | ronment is not fully | tion process stresses
 | conducive to healthy | positive mental health,
 | physical or emotional | preparation for present
 | development, they are | and future roles, and
 | not in imminent danger. | the acquisition of social
 | | skills.

II. Specific Criteria

A. FAMILY RELATIONSHIPS AND FAMILY UNITY

1. *Marital Relationship*

In cases where the marital relationship or consensual union does not fit the accepted definition it *should be checked* where either or both of the following are applicable: 1) One partner has legal responsibility toward the other, has at least some contact with the family or exerts some influence on it; 2) There is a continuing extramarital relationship of significance in family functioning.

When rating a family headed by an O.W. (out-of-wedlock) mother, code the relationship between the unmarried mother and the father of her child(ren). However, if there is a sustained, ongoing relationship between her and any other "significant male" (other than members of her family) rate the quality of that relationship. (A "significant" other is one with whom there is a continuing, emotional relationship and who asserts some influence on the family system.)

Check *Not Applicable* wherever above elements are not present.

INADEQUATE	MARGINAL	ADEQUATE
Partner, whether or not separated, does not support them when so ordered or is extremely disturbing influence on family.	Partner, whether or not separated, does not support adequately or is a disturbing influence on family.	Couple live together, derive satisfaction from their relationship.
Extramarital relations are endangering children's welfare, or have come to attention of law.	Extramarital relations exist but do not openly affect welfare of children, or pose immediate threat to family solidarity.	There is a positive emotional tie between partners, who can both express need for the other's help and respond appropriately when the other requires help. Considerable pleasure is derived from shared experiences.
Emotional tie so deficient that children are endangered.	Weak emotional tie between partners, lack of concern for each other.	
Severe, persistent marital conflict necessitates intervention by authorities or threatens a complete disruption of family life.	There are some points of agreement between partners, but disagreement and conflict tend to predominate.	There is a consistent effort to limit the scope and duration of marital conflict and to keep communication open for resolution of conflicts which arise.

2. *Relationship Between Parents and Children*

INADEQUATE	MARGINAL	ADEQUATE
No affection is shown between parents and	Affection between parents and children is in-	Affection is shown between parents and chil-

children. There is great indifference or marked rejection of children. No respect is shown for one another. No approval, recognition, or encouragement is shown to children. If any concern is shown at all by parents, it takes the form of rank discrimination in favor of a few against the rest. Parent-child conflict is extremely severe. (Above so serious as to constitute neglect or abuse as legally defined, warranting community intervention.)

termittent, or weak, or obscured by conflict. Parents' anger is unpredictable and unrelated to specific conduct of children. Family members are played off against each other. There is marked favoritism with no attempt to compensate disadvantaged children. There is little mutual respect or concern for each other. Parents and children are frequently in conflict. Parents of very young children are indifferent in handling or assuming responsibility for them. (Danger to children is potential not actual.)

dren. Parents try always to be consistent in treatment of children. Children have sense of belonging, emotional security. Children and parents show respect for each other, mutual concern. Parent-child conflict is minimal or restricted by consistent attention, free communication, and desire for harmony. Parents of very young children derive satisfaction from caring for them, and assume major role in their care.

3. *Sibling Relationships*

Pertains only to relationships among natural or adopted siblings.

INADEQUATE	MARGINAL	ADEQUATE
There is conflict between children resulting in physical violence or cruelty that warrants intervention.	Emotional ties among children are weak. Rarely play together. Fighting occurs, often teasing, bullying, other types of emotional or physical cruelty. Children rarely share playthings, show little loyalty to one another or pride in other's achievements.	There are positive emotional ties and mutual identification among children. Depending on age, often play together, share their playthings. Are loyal to each other, enjoy other's company, take pride in achievements of their siblings. Fighting and bickering are normal for age.

4. *Family Solidarity*

In families headed by O.W. mothers the concept covers the relationship between the mother and her natural child(ren). In addition, her relationship to her parents (natural, step, or surrogate) is covered *providing they live in the same household.* If the unmarried mother lives with other family members, code under *Relationship with Other Household Members.* Relationships with extended family not living in same household are rated under *Informal Associations.*

INADEQUATE	MARGINAL	ADEQUATE
There is marked lack of affection and emotional ties among family members. Conflict among members is persistent or severe. There is marked lack of cohesiveness and mutual concern; satisfactions in family living are not evident. There is no pride in family or sense of family identity. Members plan on basis of personal gratification rather than for family as whole. There is serious danger of family disruption. (Above is so serious that laws relating to neglect or cruelty are violated or family welfare is so threatened that intervention is justified.) Family solidarity assumes antisocial forms.	Little emotional warmth is evidenced among family members. Family members are often in conflict. There is little cohesiveness; for example, membes rarely do things together; there is little planning toward common family goals; little feeling of collective responsibility; little pulling together in crisis. There are few satisfactions in family living. (Above potential but not yet actual danger to welfare of children.)	Warmth and affection are shown among family members, giving them a sense of belonging and emotional security. Conflict within family is dealt with quickly and appropriately. There is definitive evidence of cohesiveness; for example, members often do things together; eat together, family plans and works toward some common goals; there is definite feeling of collective responsibility; members pull together in times of stress. Members find considerable satisfaction in family living. Cohesiveness is not at odds with the welfare of the community.

5. *Relationships with Other Household Members*

INADEQUATE	MARGINAL	ADEQUATE
Relationships are marked by hostilities, sometimes resulting in physical and verbal battles. The purloining of each other's personal property, disregard of privacy, or frequent fighting has resulted in, or warrants, outside intervention. Household members studiously ignore one another or treat each other with contempt. Various cruelties result in serious emotional or physical injuries to one or more household members. Conflict among children is severe, persistent, and violent. Adults show marked preference for one child over another, resulting in serious deprivation and problems warranting community intervention. Parents strongly resent presence of children in home and openly show their hostilities.	Household members resent one another's presence, and do not respect other adults' rights to privacy. Disputes are frequent, shown either by verbal bickering, petty jealousy, or ignoring of one another. Some adults refuse to take responsibilities for household, such as contributing their share to general expenses or helping with household chores, to the resentment of others. Children rarely play together or share playthings. Fighting among children is frequent but does not result in physical harm to one another. Adults show little concern or affection for children, barely tolerate their presence in household.	Adults in household group treat each other with consideration and mutual concern. Conflicts and misunderstandings are usually recognized and settled quickly and appropriately. Children in household group like to play together, don't mind sharing toys, sports equipment, etc. Disputes and bickering among children are not out of line for their age group. Adults in household group do not show favoritism or marked preference for some child(ren) over others. Adults do not mind the presence of children in household.

B. INDIVIDUAL BEHAVIOR AND ADJUSTMENT

1. *Individual Behavior and Adjustment of Parents*

Check separately for mother and father. Check "Not Applicable" (N.A.) if absent parent has no tie to family (as indicated

under marital relationship). If there are more than one mother
or father figure with ties to family, check the one who has the
strongest tie. Check "inadequate" if consequences of law
violations (incarceration, probation, etc.) are still operative;
prolonged probation should be weighted with other factors.

For Unmarried Mothers:

Father: Should be rated only if there had been a rating in the
          subcategory *Marital Relationships*. "Father" again
          pertains to either the biological father of the O.W.
          child, or a "significant" other as defined in *Marital
          Relationship*.

Mother: The presence of an out-of-wedlock child is not in
          itself a basis for a lower rating on the mother. In this
          subcategory we are rating the mother's behavior and
          her functioning in various roles, such as parent,
          homemaker, member of the community, etc., all of
          which contribute to the numerical rating of the oth-
          er's Individual Behavior and Adjustment.

INADEQUATE	MARGINAL	ADEQUATE
Social Behavior	*Social Behavior*	*Social Behavior*
Is incarcerated or on probation for law violation. Seriously deviant sexual behaviour (rape, etc.) or serious offenses against family (assault, incest, etc.) endanger welfare of children. Excessive drinking, consumption of drugs severely affects family welfare (reducing budget below minimal level, causing severe conflict, etc.) and warrants intervention for sake of children.	Minor law violations do not result in incarceration or probation; there are instances of deviant sexual conduct, offenses against family, or excessive drinking and taking of drugs, but they do not seriously affect family welfare. Deficiency in social skills handicaps comfortable relationships to people and institutions.	Law violations are limited to such slight infractions as minor traffic violations. Has good supplement of social skills, relates comfortably to most people and institutions.

Mental-Physical

Serious mental illness requires intervention or results in institutionalization. Profound and chronic unhappiness.

Mental defectiveness requires institutionalization or so limits capacity as to disrupt family life; special help or training is needed but not provided.

Parent has disease that endangers public health and entitles health authorities to intervene; has not sought or carried through on treatment; chronic or major physical disease or handicap is so disabling that person is unable to provide minimum care for children who are his/her major responsibility.

Mental-Physical

Mental or emotional disorder is present but individual functions on minimal level, not actually dangerous to family; little personal satisfaction is experienced in life. Individual is forced to function below potential.

Chronic or major physical disease or handicap is somewhat disabling but permits minimal functioning, especially in regard to care of children.

Mental-Physical

Mental health good, has positive self image. Psychosocial functioning is at the level of individual's potential. Is satisfied with situation and social roles. Has a sense of fulfillment.

Performs up to mental capacity and is able to function satisfactorily in most areas.

No diseases or handicaps of serious nature; receiving appropriate treatment, where necessary; functioning hampered only slightly if at all.

*Role Performance:**

As Spouse: If deserted or separated, does not support when so or-

*Role Performance:**

As Spouse: There is frequent conflict or disagreement with spouse

*Role Performance:**

As Spouse: Conflict with spouse is minimal, dealt with appropriately;

---

*Due allowance should be made for variations in parental roles made necessary by the particular family structure. Thus the mother's role as supplementary or chief wage earner needs to be considered where children do not have to be looked after during the day. The father's role as homemaker may have to be taken into account where he is unable to earn a living or chooses to stay home to assume a domestic role.

dered. Extramarital liaisons endanger family. Severe conflict with spouse is damaging to children.

in many areas of living; emotional tie is weak.

there is positive emotional tie; disagreements are well handled or well tolerated.

As Parent: There is violation of laws relating to neglect of children, assault, incest, etc., making intervention necessary.

As Parent: There is little concern for or interest in children. Displays little affection for them; minimal physical and emotional care are provided. Some favoritism is shown.

As Parent: There is positive relationship with children; shows them affection, spends time with them, provides appropriate physical and emotional care.

As Breadwinner: If absent, does not support when so ordered. If at home, and physically and mentally able to work, is unwilling to support family.

As Breadwinner: Provides minimal or uncertain income, but little or no P.A. required (unless so disabled as to require outside support).

As Breadwinner: Provides income for family that meets their needs satisfactorily. Works regularly at job, has positive feeling for it.

As Homemaker: Housekeeping and care of children is so inadequate that it constitutes neglect and warrants intervention.

As Homemaker: Housekeeping and care of children are generally poor, and person is uninterested in homemaker role.

As Homemaker: Housekeeping and care of children are good, and person derives satisfaction from homemaker role.

As Member of Community: There are law violations other than offenses against family. Extremely hostile attitude toward community—children are encouraged to commit antisocial acts.

As Member of Community: Has little or no social contacts with neighbors, relatives, etc.; belongs to no social groups, is dissatisfied with social status. Makes poor use of resources, is ignorant of, or apathetic toward, resources when need exists to use them.

As Member of Community: Has meaningful ties with friends, relatives, etc. Belongs to some social groups that provide satisfactions, is comfortable with standing in community. Has positive attitude toward community, makes good use of facilities when necessary. Strivings toward upward mobility are kept within realistic bounds.

2. *Individual Behavior and Adjustment of Children*

For purposes of scoring, children 10 and over are considered together, as are children from 1 to 9. The total score for each group is determined by finding the weighted average of separate scores. Do not consider children who are *permanently* out of the home. Rate only the natural or adoptive children of the nuclear family or unmarried mother. (In studies that focus on the functioning of the children, each child should be rated separately for purposes of furnishing score outputs in which each sibling can be treated as a variable. For a more detailed rating of children see Appendix B.)

INADEQUATE	MARGINAL	ADEQUATE
Acting-Out Behavior:	*Acting-Out Behavior:*	*Acting-Out Behavior:*
Acting out, disruptive, antisocial behavior is of serious concern and indicative of a child in real danger, warranting intervention. Incarcerated or on probation.	Acting out, disruptive, or antisocial behavior is not a long or continuous pattern.	Acting-out behavior is normal for age; pranks, mischievousness, etc., not of serious nature.
Mental-Physical State:	*Mental-Physical State:*	*Mental-Physical State:*
Mental illness requires intervention or results in hospitalization. Excessive withdrawal, heavy drinking, drug addiction, or other behavior suggests emotional disturbance or serious problems in relating to others.	Emotional disorder is evident, but receiving treatment or not serious enough to justify intervention; little personal satisfaction is experienced in life.	Emotional health appears good, has positive self-image, enjoys appropriate activities, relates well to others, is satisfied with his/her life.
Mental defectiveness is present requiring in-	Performance is below mental and/or physical capacity. Mental retardation severely limits functioning, but special	Performs up to mental and physical capacity and is able to function well in most areas.

stitutional training or custodial care that is not provided.

Child has disease that endangers public health; no measures are taken for isolation or treatment. Other serious health conditions or handicaps are present for which proper care is not provided.

training, such as special class, is received.

Child not retarded but performs well below capacity.

Chronic or major physical disease or handicap is present; receives some treatment, but permits minimal functioning.

Diseases or handicaps, if present, are receiving appropriate care with resulting favorable adjustment.

Role Performance:

Role Performance:

Role Performance:

As Child: There is violent, destructive, or assaultive behavior against family members.

As Child: Gets along poorly with parents and siblings, rarely performs household or other duties expected of him/her.

As Child: There are close ties to family members. Continuously participates in household duties and family life.

As Pupil: Excessive truancy, disruptiveness, incorrigibility, or property destruction necessitates intervention. Other infringements of school regulations result in suspension, expulsion, etc.

As Pupil: Acting-out or withdrawn behavior is of less serious nature. Attendance is not regular but no action is taken. Schoolwork is poor. There is little positive feeling toward school.

As Pupil: Attends regularly; schoolwork approximates ability; there is positive attitude toward school. Acting out is limited to occasional pranks.

As Peer: Participates with others in delinquent acts. Inability to relate to peers suggests severe emotional disturbance. Is often involved in severe conflicts with peers.

As Peer: Has few friends; is in frequent conflict with peers; associates with groups whose behavior is not acceptable to immediate community.

As Peer: Is well liked; has friends; participates satisfactorily in peer groups.

C. CARE AND TRAINING OF CHILDREN

1. *Physical Care*

INADEQUATE	MARGINAL	ADEQUATE
Supply and care of clothes, cleanliness, diet, and health care for children are seriously deficient, endangers their health or threatens adjustment in school and acceptance in peer groups. Vermin is a serious health or social handicap. (Above is so serious that intervention is warranted.)	Children do not receive proper diet, their sleep schedule is irregular and insufficient for their needs. Sleeping quarters are crowded, parents are indifferent and lax in providing suitable exercise or recreational outlets for children. Clothing is in short supply, poorly maintained— personal hygiene neglected.	Children's diet is nutritious; provisions are made for sufficient sleep and exercise. Children have suitable clothes, adequate sleeping space, and are kept clean. Health needs (preventive and remedial) are looked after promptly and appropriately.

2. *Training Methods and Emotional Care*

INADEQUATE	MARGINAL	ADEQUATE
Affection is rarely shown to children; there is marked indifference or obvious rejection. Parents have pathological tie to children, use them as pawns. Physical and emotional cruelty is present. (Above is so serious that intervention is warranted.)	Little affection is shown to children; parents are usually indifferent to or reject children, or are overly permissive. Children have little sense of emotional security. (Above is not of imminent danger to children.)	Parents show steady affection for children, provide atmosphere of emotional warmth, sense of belonging.
Parents' behavior standards are so deviant from wider community that children are encouraged toward antisocial acts.	Parents' behavior standards are in many respects somewhat deviant from community, or there is a lack of standards, or parents expect too much or too little maturity.	Parents' ideas of how children should behave are generally those acceptable to the community. Standards of behavior are appropriate to age level.
		Methods used are usually appropriate to behavior. Approval of good conduct is often shown. Parents are fairly con-

Physical punishment is overly severe or inappropriate. There is extreme lack of discipline. There is inconsistency of methods in one parent or between parents, limits are not enforced, strong disagreement exists between parents on training. Approval is shown rarely or not at all. (Above directly contributes to delinquent behavior or otherwise puts children in danger.)

Parents are overly rigid, over-permissive, indifferent. Physical punishment, swearing occurs. Discipline is not appropriate to behavior. Approval of good conduct is rare. Parents are inconsistent, often do not enforce limits, disagree with each other over exercise of discipline, do not share task of training. Parents show favoritism. (Above is potential rather than actual danger)

sistent in exercising discipline, enforce limits set, agree with each other in exercising discipline, share job of training children.

D. SOCIAL ACTIVITIES

1. *Informal Associations*

INADEQUATE

Conflict with relatives, neighbors, friends results in physical violence or illegal activities. Persons as above are such a disturbing and discordant influence on family as to endanger welfare of children. Friends participate in perpetrating delinquent antisocial acts.

MARGINAL

There are broken, discordant, or indifferent relationships with relatives, squabbles with neighbors. Family members have few or no social outlets with friends or have friends whose influence leads to dubious social consequences (drunken sprees, consumption of drugs, destruction of property, children left alone, etc.)

ADEQUATE

Majority of relationships with relatives and friends are pleasant and satisfying. Amicable relationships maintained with neighbors. Family members have social outlets, appropriate to stage of family development, providing recreational and interpersonal satisfactions, sense of identification with larger groups, and necessary socialization experiences for children. Marital partners agree on how leisure time is to be spent.

2. *Formal Associations*

Rate N.A. if there are no formal associations and respondents have no opinions, or only neutral attitudes, about formal associations. Where there is a need to belong to a formal association and a refusal to do so, the rating must be less than adequate. If negative views are expressed but no formal associations are in evidence, rate this subcategory but not below "marginal."

Belonging to one organization, such as a labor union, does not necessarily qualify for an "adequate" rating. Into your judgment here must enter considerations on understanding the nature of organization, quality of participation, and general attitude toward the organization.

Church membership alone does not qualify for a rating in this subcategory; however, being active in a church-sponsored group or club does.

INADEQUATE	MARGINAL	ADEQUATE
There is membership in formal groups perpetrating antisocial acts. Behavior in organized group is so destructive or disruptive that intervention is necessary.	Family feels socially alone and unable to improve social status. In contrast to other families in the community or status group, family members belong to no organized groups.	Family members, where appropriate, belong to some clubs, organizations, etc., participate in some activities and derive satisfaction from belonging. Some members are active in groups that lend support to community betterment.

E.   ECONOMIC PRACTICES

1.   *Source and Amount of Income*

If family is headed by an O.W. mother who lives with her parents or other members of her extended family and is com-

pletely dependent upon them economically, the family income
is rated. If the O.W. mother subsists on her own income (could
be AFDC grant), even if she lives with her family, her income
is rated independently of others. If part of the O.W. mother's
income is her own, and part from her family, the focus is still
on the adequacy of funds as it pertains to the O.W. mother and
her children. In this instance, the income from her family may
be seen as coming from an outside source, such as a pension,
insurance, gifts, etc.

INADEQUATE	MARGINAL	ADEQUATE
Amount of income is so low or unstable that basic necessities are not provided for family members.	Amount of income is marginal or unstable, barely meets family needs.	Family is financially sufficiently independent to afford a few luxuries or savings, is fairly well satisfied with economic status, and is working toward greater financial security.
Family is frequently deprived of source of income because of failure of able-bodied family members to support. Income from Public Assistance is obtained through fraudulent means. Income is derived from theft, forgery, etc.	Income is derived from general relief or Public Assistance. Children in home, though of working age and not in school, are not employed or contributing to family income. Family is dissatisfied with amount of income.	Income is derived from work of family members, or from such sources as pensions, insurances, rent, support payments, etc., but money is not from public-welfare funds.

2. *Job Situation*

Applies only to family members contributing substantially to
support of family. If the unmarried mother is not employed
because she has to care for her children, always rate N.A. Treat
temporary or seasonal lay-offs (as in construction business) as
if wage earner were employed.

INADEQUATE	MARGINAL	ADEQUATE
Law-breaking behavior is exhibited on job, such	There are frequent changes of job, unsteady	Works regularly at full-time job, seeks im-

as fraud, embezzlement, robbery, physical violence to co-workers.

Able-bodied man unwilling to obtain employment.

work patterns; the employee works less than full time, job is below capacity. There are poor relations with employer and co-workers and dissatisfaction with job.

provement if not fully satisfied, changes jobs only when it is unavoidable due to economic or other circumstances, or for improvement. Job is suitable for capabilities; worker maintains harmonious relations with employer and co-workers, and has positive feeling toward job.

3. *Use of Money*

INADEQUATE	MARGINAL	ADEQUATE
Severe conflict over control of income endangers children's welfare. Budgeting and money management are so poor that basic necessities are not provided. Excessive debt results in legal action.	Disagreement over control of income leads to conflict or dissatisfaction among family members. Family is unable to live within budget, money management is poor, luxuries take precedence over basic necessities, there is impulsive spending. (Above do not seriously endanger family's welfare.)	Money is spent on the basis of agreement that such is responsibility of one or more members of family. Family budgets income; money management is carried out with realistic regard to basic necessities. Debts are manageable and planned for in budget.

F. HOME AND HOUSEHOLD PRACTICES

1. *Physical Facilities*

INADEQUATE	MARGINAL	ADEQUATE
Property is in deteriorated condition, kept in very poor state of re-	Property is deteriorating and in need of repair, or sufficient space	Property is kept in good condition; there is sufficient space for family

pair. Facilities for sleeping, washing, sanitation, heat, water, refrigeration, or cooking are so inadequate as to be an actual threat to the physical and emotional welfare of family members, particularly children, and necessitate intervention by health or other authorities.

Homes and stores along street are in advanced state of deterioration. Trash, garbage, abandoned cars, various junk objects are scattered along streets and vacant lots, create a health hazard to the residents. Area is not considered "safe" after dark. Among loiterers on street and in doorways one can identify "skid-row" elements, such as alcoholics, dope addicts, hustlers, etc. There are no play areas for youngsters, or if such exist, they are dangerous to the welfare of children.

is not available. There is absence or inadequacy of basic household equipment. (Above potentially harmful to welfare of children.)

Homes and stores along streets are in poor state of repair. Streets are poorly maintained; there are not enough play areas for children, who either have to play on sidewalks or go a great distance to a park or playground. Heavy automobile traffic makes it potentially dangerous for children to cross street or play on sidewalks. A home along a busy main thoroughfare, which may be satisfactory for adults, constitutes a potential danger area for young children. Home in close proximity to factories that create noise and pollute the air.

members. Necessary household equipment is available and in good working order. Family members are satisfied and pleased with their home.

Streets and sidewalks are kept clean and in good condition. There is sufficient illumination, and streets are "safe" to walk on, both day and night. Play and recreational areas for children are available within short walking distance. Neighborhood usually designated as "residential" and consists mainly of dwelling units in good state of repair and upkeep.

2.　*Housekeeping Standards*

INADEQUATE	MARGINAL	ADEQUATE
Home is maintained in such a dirty and unsanitary condition, meals are so irregular, diet is	Home is in disorder, meals are irregular, diet is poorly planned, making a potential hazard	Home is maintained in a condition conducive to good health, hygiene, and a sense of orderli-

so inadequate as to con-
stitute an actual hazard
to physical well-being of
family members. Ver-
min or rats present se-
rious health hazard.

to physical welfare of
family members.

ness. Meals are served
regularly, diet is well
balanced and nutritious.
Attention is paid to
making home attractive
and pleasant to family
members.

G.   HEALTH CONDITIONS AND PRACTICES

1.   *Health Conditions*

Minor mental disorders and maladjustment are *not* to be considered here, but evaluated under *Individual Behavior and
Adjustment.*

Inadequate	Marginal	Adequate
Presence of communicable disease endangers public health; patient is not isolated or properly treated. Major physical or mental illness or chronic disease or handicap so severely limits person's functioning within and outside the home that there is an actual threat to family welfare, particularly the care children are receiving.	Disease, chronic illness, or handicaps limit person's functioning inside and outside home, but it constitutes no actual threat to family welfare.	Physical and mental health of family members are such that they are able to function satisfactorily in their various roles. Good health, including condition of teeth, is generally apparent.

2.   *Health Practices*

Inadequate	Marginal	Adequate
Proper treatment or quarantine is not se-	There is refusal or failure to get or continue	Concern is shown about ill health or handicaps,

cured for diseases endangering life of person and/or public health. Parents neglect or refuse to provide medical or other remedial care for health and wellbeing of children. Disease-prevention practices (sanitation, diet, etc.) are not followed. Conditions are so poor that physical neglect of children is involved.

medical care for minor ailments. Medical instructions are disregarded or not followed consistently. Disease-prevention practices are not generally followed, but health of family members is not seriously endangered.

medical care is promptly sought when needed, medical instructions are followed.

Disease-prevention and dental-hygiene practices are observed.

H.   RELATIONSHIP TO INTERVENTION WORKER

Rate N.A. unless there is a professional relationship of significance between an intervention worker and family life.

1.   *Attitude Toward Worker*

INADEQUATE	MARGINAL	ADEQUATE
There is physical violence or verbal assault and other types of threatening or insulting behavior.	Worker is met with suspicion, resentment, or defensiveness on part of family, or marked indifference.	Worker is received with friendliness or affective neutrality, with readiness to consider family problems in relation to services offered.

2.   *Use of Worker*

INADEQUATE	MARGINAL	ADEQUATE
There is refusal to talk with worker when the basis of community concern is such that the worker has a right to	Client is reluctant to engage in social-work relationship and to recognize and/or deal with problems that face	Client shows willingness to engage in a positive social-work relationship, and to work toward enhancing or

stay in the situation. There is absolute refusal to acknowledge any problems. Deceptive and fraudulent behavior is shown toward worker.

him/her and the family. There is manipulative use of worker.

improving family's social functioning. Client freely calls on worker in pursuit of this goal.

I. USE OF COMMUNITY RESOURCES

If family has no knowledge of any health, social, and recreational resources, a "near adequate" rating, at best, can be given.

The expression of a critical opinion about any resource when that resource has shortcomings does not call for a negative rating.

If respondent has no association with social and recreational agencies, rate N.A. If there is a need for using a community resource but a refusal to do so, a less than "adequate" rating must be assigned. If respondent has no connections with, or present need for using, a community resource but expresses a negative opinion (e.g., "I heard so many terrible things about relief that I would starve first before going to them for help."), rating may be lower than "adequate" but cannot be below "marginal."

1. School

Rate parents' attitude toward schools and education, even if all children are of pre-school age.

INADEQUATE	MARGINAL	ADEQUATE
Parents are extremely hostile to school, encourage or abet consistent truancy, are an-	Parents place little value on education, take little interest in children's school activities,	Parents value education for their children, facilitate regular school attendance, are coopera-

tagonistic to school personnel, refuse to cooperate when this is made necessary by the seriousness of community concern.

Children have extremely negative attitude toward school, are excessively truant without excuse, are very disruptive, destroy school property, commit other infringements of school regulations demanding intervention.

are lax in enforcing attendance, are uncooperative with school in plans for children.

Children have negative attitude toward school, truant rather frequently, are a disruptive or disturbing influence, do poor schoolwork (but not sufficiently serious to warrant intervention).

tive with school personnel when joint planning is indicated.

Children value school, attend regularly, are not behavior problems, achieve according to capacity.

2. *Religious Institutions (Church or Synagogue)*

Check in the "adequate" to "marginal" range only if family member(s) is participating in church activities. If there are no church ties, or only nominal church membership, check N.A. "Inadequate" may, however, be checked regardless of whether family has church ties.

INADEQUATE	MARGINAL	ADEQUATE
Law violations are directed against religious institutions, such as robbery, destruction of property, committing nuisances, vandalism, etc. Instill hostile attitudes in children toward religion. Serious religious conflict between parents has negative effect upon children.	Family members are a disruptive influence in a church group. There is a little satisfaction from church or synagogue affiliation; there is conflict among family members about church attendance or participation in church sponsored activities.	Attend religious institution fairly regularly, whenever possible; derive personal satisfaction from such ties.

3. *Health Resources*

If private doctors or dentists are used, they are viewed and rated the same as any other health resource.

INADEQUATE	MARGINAL	ADEQUATE
Hostility, bitterness or apathy toward available health resources are so great that serious health problems of family members do not receive medical attention. Health needs of parents, which prevent them from caring for children, are not met.	Family regards health resources with suspicion, hostility, or resentment. Agencies are used unconstructively, appointments are missed, follow-through is lacking, medical advice is not followed, but not to the extent of seriously endangering welfare of family members.	Family has positive attitude toward health agencies and resources; available facilities are used promptly when need arises, appointments are kept, medical advice is followed.

4. *Social Agencies*

Includes correctional services, housing authority, employment agencies, welfare agencies, mental-health and social-adjustment services. If client is not using social agencies, and has no need to do so, rate N.A.

INADEQUATE	MARGINAL	ADEQUATE
There is extreme hostility to social agencies, leading to such behavior as assault, robbery, destruction of property, or fraud. There is refusal to accept agency services where this has been ordered by law or is necessary because of community concern.	Attitude toward agencies is marked by hostility, resentment, defensiveness, apathy, etc. Agencies are used unconstructively—family is not cooperative, or is apathetic, or overly demanding, etc.	Attitude toward agencies is positive. Family utilizes agencies appropriately for improvement of family life or for meeting needs of individual members, is cooperative in working on joint plans.

5. *Recreational Agencies*

Refers only to publicly sponsored facilities. Participation in commercial enterprises, like bowling alleys, amusement parks, dance-clubs, etc., will be rated under *D. Social Activities.*

INADEQUATE	MARGINAL	ADEQUATE
Hostility toward recreational agencies leads to assault, robbery, destruction of property, etc. Parents prevent children from using organized recreational facilities.	Children seldom use recreational facilities, such as playgrounds, etc. If use is made, behavior is characterized by disruptiveness, noncooperation, etc.	Family members, particularly children, make use of available recreational resources according to age and interest; resources and services provide satisfaction and necessary socialization experience for children.

5b. *The Rating Procedure*

Rating or coding is a process used to reduce qualitative or descriptive data to a quantitative (nominal, ordinal, or interval) format. Rating requires the application of judgment; it is generally guided by instructions or guidelines, which in our case are quite detailed, for the more specific the instructions the less room there is for idiosyncratic judgment on the part of the rater. Although we have attempted to minimize the introduction of subjective considerations, it is obvious that they cannot be completely eliminated. To rate family functioning one must compare a situation described in the Profile of Family Functioning with the criteria, which are descriptions at a higher level of abstraction. A certain amount of subjective judgment enters into the making of every comparison, because there is usually some discrepancy between the descriptive level and that of the criterion.

Before rating is undertaken the researcher must accept the premise that it is a theoretically justified method. The rater must understand the conceptual organization of the material, because the coding of complex narrative data, such as we have here, frequently necessitates a mental reordering of content scattered in overlapping categories. It can be assumed that knowledge of the behavioral sciences is helpful in coding, but whether a graduate education makes a better coder is a moot question. This writer with rather extensive experience has found that coders with both undergraduate and graduate training have performed with seemingly comparable results.

The following guidelines should be helpful in rating a Profile of Family Functioning:

(1)   As a first step the coder will find it helpful to keep in mind the continuum, shown below, for scoring subcategories and main categories of social functioning.

The prospective coder will notice that only the positions marked by blocks rather than lines, which represent the values *1, 4,* and *7,* have been defined in the criteria for rating family functioning shown above. The in-between positions with values *2, 3, 5,* and *6,* which are approximations to the adjacent anchor positions, are to be used when the coder has determined that a given situation does not fully correspond to the level of functioning described in the anchor position but falls instead above or below it.

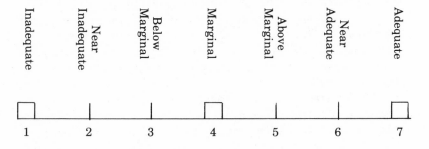

(2)   The coder should read over the criteria for rating family
functioning and study carefully the general criteria. The specific criteria should be examined closely at the time the case is
being rated.

(3)   The Profile of Family Functioning should now be read
in its entirety. For purposes of rating, a grasp of the entire
family picture is necessary, because even the best organized
protocol will have some information missing or incompletely
covered under the proper heading and placed elsewhere. The
coder who has studied the entire case will use this information
appropriately and will also be aware of the extent to which
information is completely missing from the Profile. The reading at this point should cover only the beginning situation or
first Profile. This will help avoid confusion in the mind of the
coder regarding different temporal stages in family functioning.

(4)   The next step calls for a reading and subsequent rating
of the Profile, subcategory by subcategory and area (or main
category) by area. Each group of subcategories making up an
area is rated before coding the area as a whole. Ratings are
entered in the appropriate column on the code sheet shown
on pp. 156–159. A rating will take one of three forms: a substantive or numerical area or subcategory rating in the form of a
whole number between 1 and 7; an N.K. or "not known" because
the information under a given heading is missing; and an N.A.
or "not applicable," whenever information under a given heading
is irrelevant. The latter would include the subcategory "sibling
relationships" when there is only one child, or the subcategory
"job situation" if no one in the family is employed.

(5)   The area or main-category scores are a composite of the
subcategory ratings. The former require a judgmental weighting of the latter, rather than a statistical procedure, such as
computing the mean or mode. The numerical values of sub-

categories limit the range within which area scores can be assigned. In other words, if subcategory ratings are all 4s and 5s, the area score cannot be 3 or 6 but must be either 4 or 5. The value of the final score depends upon which subcategories are dominant in describing the characteristics of the family's functioning within the total area. For instance, Care and Training of Children, which is characterized by poor "training and emotional care" (because of inconsistent discipline, cruelty, and preferential treatment of one child) but adequate "physical care," should be assigned a low area score. The coder will have to judge whether the high rating in "physical care" should result in a main-category score slightly higher than the rating for "training and emotional care." The area score might be upgraded if the coder had evidence that the good "physical care" helped reduce the harm done by inferior training and emotional care.

(6) The score for Individual Behavior and Adjustment is also a composite, and the weighting of scores of family members to be rated takes into account their influence upon family life. The score weight for a separated father who visits the family on occasion is lower than that of a mother in the home. Similarly, a baby in the crib is given a lower weight than a teenager who takes an active part in family life. Separate ratings are given for the father, mother, older children (10 years and over), and younger children (under 10 years). Coders may not wish to group children into two collective categories but rate each of them separately. If this is done, separate scores for each child according to age can be entered into their respective categories.

(7) After rating the beginning situation the coder can undertake the rating of the second Profile, if there is indeed a second one. A cross-sectional study may involve only a single evaluation of family functioning, whereas dynamic studies, either of the before-after or panel type, would have two or more

Profiles, the second of which would cover a designated time period following the beginning situation. Since the second (or subsequent) Profile was written with reference to changes occurring since the beginning situation, the rating must also be done in such a fashion. To do this the coder who scores the after situation must familiarize her- himself with the contents and the scores of the beginning Profile. Only after such preparation will the coder proceed, as was done in the first coding, by reading the narrative in the later Profile and assigning ratings according to the level of functioning criteria. A separate score sheet, identical with the first one, will be used with the appropriate ordinal Profile number checked.

(8)   Movement is the numerical difference between scores of a given Profile and those of a later one, arrived at by simply subtracting scores and entering the sum in the movement score sheet shown on pp. 164–167. Three types of movement may be differentiated: positive, zero, and negative. Positive and negative movement can range from *1* to *6,* the latter representing a situation where the change is from a score of *1* (inadequate) to 7 (adequate) or the converse.

(9)   The heuristic device of graphing the Profile of Family Functioning may be decided upon if the instrument is to be given clinical use. One chart would be employed for graphing the beginning and after (or several subsequent) situations; a second one would be used for showing movement, and an example of this will follow the case presentation below. Groups of cases can also be represented pictorially, with the graph being based on mean scores and standard deviations, which are marked off—by means of different colors or broken and straight lines—at intervals on both sides of each graph.

The following presentation of an actual case should help clarify the foregoing instructions and guidelines for profiling and rating. In recent years the St. Paul Scale of Family

Functioning has been used rather extensively to study relatively "normal" families, and this case may be said to fall under this heading. It may be recalled that the instrument was developed originally to assess the social functioning of disorganized families, and the case example presented in the first manual on measurement (Geismar and Ayres 1960) belonged to that category. However, this case study is more typical of the "normal" type of family, the kind researched in the Family Life Improvement Project, for instance, (Geismar, Lagay, Wolock, et al.) than the type of disorganized family studied by the St. Paul Family Centered Project (Geismar and Ayres 1959) or the Chemung County Study (Brown).

The case presented below constitutes a study of change by virtue of the fact that two separate Profiles are shown, describing social functioning over an eighteen-month period. For easier comparison the beginning and after situation are juxtaposed on the same page rather than on separate pages as recommended in the instructions. The family described here has been receiving professional social-work services for child-behavior and marital problems. Movement in family functioning, as the reader will notice, coincides with positive changes in treatment. However, the Profile writer does not assume any cause-and-effect relationship between service and movement in social functioning. On the contrary, a careful reading of the Profile will show that many important changes were due to circumstances beyond the reach of the professional intervener, such as the improved employment situation resulting from the establishment of a new family business. Yet, other positive changes, particularly in the childrearing process, might be traced more directly to the activities of the social worker.

This case study of the Z. family is, in fact, a good illustration of the complex interrelationship between intervention programs on the one hand, and change in family functioning on the other. Efforts aimed at providing something approximating a causal nexus must be devoted to meeting such requirements of experimental design building as hypothesizing the specific changes anticipated as a result of services and setting up one or more matched control groups to check the effects of nonexperimental variables on family functioning.

The Z. family, as both the narrative and the score Profile will show, is not particularly problematic. Social functioning is above the marginal coordinate defined as the level at which behavior may be said to be potentially threatening to the welfare of family members or the community. On the other hand, there are several areas and subareas where functioning is near marginal, denoting dissatisfactions, stresses, and strains in family life. Adequate or near-adequate functioning in the after situation denotes concrete though not spectacular improvement over an eighteen-month period. The essential dynamic of the Z.'s functioning is in the narrative, not the score Profile. The latter represents—as does all quantitative research—a form of data reduction that makes the loss of some content inevitable. The conceptual organization of scores, nonetheless, makes the numerical Profile quite meaningful without a spelling out of the content of areas and subcategories. But while the numerical or graphic family Profile may have some clinical uses, its essential value resides in its potential for making the study of family functioning a scientific enterprise in which hypotheses can be tested and theories developed.

5c.   The Z. Family as an Example of Profiling and Rating Family Functioning

A.   FAMILY RELATIONSHIPS AND UNITY

    1.   *Marital Relationship*

       a.   *History*

The young couple met at a fraternity party at an eastern state university when Mrs. Z. was 19 and Mr. Z. was 23 and in service. There was no formal engagement for there was very little time between the initial meeting and their marriage. He saw her during his brief leave, wrote to her from his base, and proposed after a few letters. Mrs. Z. was impressed by his service affiliation and officer's rank (second lieutenant), by his age, and by his extroverted manner and competence as master of ceremonies at the fraternity dance. Mr. Z. liked her outgoing and decisive personality and the easy popularity she seemed to enjoy. Mr. Z.'s father (his mother had died when he was eight), who was a storekeeper in a small town in Delaware, was glad he found a Jewish bride. Mrs. Z. had had a promiscuous past, for which she had received therapy. Her father, afraid that she was known to be "fast" in their community, a medium-sized city in New Jersey, and therefore unacceptable to most of the families there, advised her to marry this out-of-town boy, and she took his advice. They arranged a military wedding near his base in Texas.

The Z.'s set up housekeeping in a small apartment off base, far from family and in a part of the country that was new and strange to them. Mr. Z. was gone on training flights for long periods of time, leaving his young wife alone with a few other army wives for company. They decided to have a child as quickly as possible. Shortly after their first child, a boy, was born, Mr. Z. was discharged from the service. Returning to his hometown, Mr. Z. found a job in a nearby city as a radio announcer, a position for which he had been trained. But another child was on its way, and he found the pay meager with little chance of advancement. They moved, then, to her hometown, which was larger and where employment seemed a little more promising.

There followed a period of a year in which Mr. Z. tried to sell insurance. But the personality difficulties that his wife had first observed in Texas—passivity, lethargy, general lack of self-discipline and aggressiveness—hindered him. He would often become depressed and sit idly at home while weeks drifted by and income ceased. Increasingly, Mrs. Z. found herself making the decisions about housing, purchases, payment or deferment of bills. Her father told her that she would have to take over and be the decisive one in the family. It was during this period, in fact, that Mrs. Z. became much closer to her father, using him both as a confidant to whom she could complain about her husband and an adviser who could help her manage the household. Mr. Z., on the other hand, found in his father-in-law the father he had never had, for he had been reared by an aunt. The father-in-law's protection and advice were actively sought by Mr. Z., while at the same time he expressed the desire to impress him by making a great deal of money in the insurance business.

During this period they saw few people besides the family. Mr. Z.'s father had remarried but Mr. Z. refused to have anything to do with his stepmother. Mrs. Z. intervened, convinced her husband that they should drive down with the children and visit over the weekend, and, on the pretext of introducing the boys to their grandmother, helped her husband accept the new family member. They often visited with Mrs. Z.'s parents (the L.'s) and extended family but did not see many of the friends Mrs. Z. had made as a teenager.

From the beginning the couple's sexual patterns had been problematic. Mr. Z. was upset about his wife's lack of response. Learning that she had had intimacies before marriage, he felt her apparent coldness was a reaction to him. Mrs. Z., however, insisted that sexual relationships had never been satisfying for her. After the two boys were born in quick succession, they used a diaphragm to thwart further conception. Mrs. Z. often expressed the wish that they had waited before having children.

On the whole, Mr. Z. gave evidence of being content with his family. He seemed pleased with the home and the routine and ties it provided. Mrs. Z., on the other hand, resented the amount of initiative she had to take in financial matters and her husband's lack of help in keeping house or caring for children. She was embarrassed at their shabby apartment and her lack of clothing and distressed over her husband's failure to make a living. In her teens when she had not responded in her first sexual encounters there had been little anxiety, but now she was upset by her apparent frigidity.

The first child had come within the first year of marriage, and Mrs. Z. had been very pleased by the pregnancy, which set her apart from her young friends. On a short trip home from Texas she had preened herself in the eyes of family and friends. The arrival of the child, however, found her unprepared for the responsibility and demands it brought. Her mother (Mrs. L.) flew down to help her but, indecisive and unwell, she proved to be of little help. The baby had long periods of crying, which tired the young mother, but Mr. Z. did not realize that he could or should be of help and spent most of the leave (which had been arranged to coincide with the birth) watching television. The pattern of noninvolvement persisted. Mrs. Z. retained responsibility for child care even at times of illness or when her husband was idle, and she was very resentful of this.

Mr. Z. was very proud of his son at birth but became less interested in him as he grew older. Essentially the same could be said for the second child. Mrs. Z. found them a source of pride but also seemed worn out from trying to cope with them.

A.1.b. *Present Functioning*

Mr. and Mrs. Z. enjoy similar recreational activities (baseball, bowling) and like the same types of movies and television programs. They both would enjoy active memberships in social and

A.1.b. *Present Functioning*

Some eighteen months later there is less tension in the household, probably a result of Mr. Z.'s new job. No longer on his own in a selling position, he now works for his father-in-law in a fraternal organizations and wish they had more leisure time to pursue these.

Mrs. Z. is a strong-willed, quick-tempered, decisive woman, while Mr. Z. is a sociable, eager-to-please, dependent man with a fund of jokes and tall tales. Mrs. Z. indicates that she would like to make fewer of the family's financial decisions and is resentful of being pushed into the dominant position. Mr. Z., who has a tendency to become depressed and then immobile, retreats from her anger when she "blows up" and defends himself by becoming silent or preoccupied. He covers up for inadequacies by lying and finds himself unable to talk out their marital difficulties.

Presently, Mr. Z. is employed selling house-to-house for a national firm, but he is not happy with the job or his performance. Although he seems to have a salesman's outgoing personality and does well in initial contacts, his selling record is erratic, he does not win sales con-

newly bought surburban liquor store. With a closely supervised structure of hours and tasks and assured clients, there has been no recurrence of depression. Thus, one of the main triggers to Mrs. Z.'s spells of vocal anger has been removed.

Mrs. Z. continues to make most of the household decisions, but she is acknowledging now that she enjoys doing it. Mr. Z., however, was the moving force in planning their first vacation this summer. He chose the site (Shenandoah Forest), decided to rent a camper, and mapped out their route. Mr. Z. is attempting to help with the children and chores, sometimes disposing of the garbage, drying dishes, bathing the children when his time allows. It is still difficult for him to acknowledge or talk out marital problems, and he continues to retreat from direct conversations about this with his wife. Mrs. Z. is less unhappy about caring for the house now that Mr. Z. is working under structured circumstances.

tests, he has not been promoted to district manager, and, most important, his take-home pay fluctuates widely from week to week. He has never attained his goal of becoming successful by making a great deal of money.

The people they see are those who come to the occasional club meetings the Z.'s attend and the bimonthly bowling league that is mandatory for firm members. Mrs. Z. is embarrassed by her small house and does not invite her old friends to her home. She cannot pay a sitter but does take off a few times a month to play mah jongg when her mother comes to relieve her. At these times Mrs. L. usually cleans the house—especially the kitchen—which is never kept clean. Their main form of socializing is visiting the L.'s three or four times a week. There are a number of family members—sisters, aunts, and cousins—with professional or successful business positions to whom the Z.'s feel inferior. They do

The home is usually clean and, although not tidy at all times, it no longer offends her mother.

Mrs. Z. is attempting to become less involved with her own extended family, especially her father, although this is difficult because the job situation forces them into close contact. The Z.'s decided to buy furniture for the living room without prior consultation with the L.'s, and the wife is trying to stop her habit of complaining to them about her husband. The Z.'s have decided to limit their visits with the L.'s to Sunday. The wife has discouraged unexpected visits by her parents by leaving the house to do chores when they dropped by. Increasingly, the Z.'s are attempting to create a social group of peers. She has invited old friends with husbands to dinner twice in the last two months (she explains that they now have a dining-room set) and her sewing club is planning to have a party in their recreation room next week.

not cease taking part in family activities on this account, however. The family's long-range goal is to make enough money to buy a larger house, to be as financially successful and secure as other members of their family and social class.

As was mentioned before, Mrs. Z. decides how the weekly check is to be handled, when to pay debts, what purchases to make. She is not reconciled to this responsibility and has told her husband so. She makes the decisions about child care, securing medical services, and their occasional social activities. Buying the house was a joint decision, with Mrs. Z. taking the lead and her father supporting their decision. The second car was also a joint purchase, but without the in-laws consent. The Z.'s felt there should be another car to use during the day when their first one is needed for selling. On the whole, though, whenever they are faced with a difficult decision, Mrs. Z. takes

Mr. Z. still has little confidence in himself. The liquor store had trouble with the police when he unintentionally sold beer to a minor and then repeated the same offense a few weeks later. His father-in-law reprimanded him severely, for it meant losing their license for a short time. Mr. L. has forbidden him to make policy decisions; Mrs. Z. feels this is just as well since she questions his ability to do so. On the other hand, customers ask for Mr. Z. if Mr. L. is in the store, for they enjoy his friendly manner. Mr. L. has attempted to give him credit for this popularity, which is essential if the store is to survive.

In the beginning, Mrs. Z. was involved in the new business, staying in the store late in the evenings while her husband made deliveries, a service they hoped would increase business. (Mrs. L. was too ill to help and Mr. L. had another job at that time, trusting Mr. Z. to be the store's manager.) But Mrs. Z. deeply resented this demand upon her at a time when her children were at home and had to eat supper.

the initiative after asking her father for advice.

While Mr. Z. supports the family, he relies upon his wife to keep the sales accounts and to help him pack merchandise to fill the orders. A number of nights a week must be devoted to putting orders together and checking the accounts. Mrs. Z. has, at times, helped her husband by delivering the goods, thus freeing him to do more selling. But through all these acts of cooperation runs a thread of anger, which is exhibited in eruptions of shouting and arguments whenever she considers too much time is being taken in this fashion to the detriment of the children or the running of the household. She feels too many tasks are allotted to her and that her husband does not carry responsibility for enough areas.

Their sexual adjustment stands as described under *History;* he is defensive and feels he is a failure, while she is anxious and worried about her lack of response.

Sometimes the children were left alone to feed themselves if a sitter were unavailable. This practice was discontinued when Mr. L.'s other job was terminated, and the two men began caring for the store together.

The Z.'s seem to have found a partial solution to their sexual problems. They have found that Mrs. Z. can respond if there is prolonged foreplay and special positions are used. However, Mrs. Z. feels somewhat guilty about this, and it is doubtful that this can long satisfy Mr. Z.'s determination to prove his ability with her.

A.2. *Relationship Between Parents and Children*

There is not much display of affection between parents and children. The mother directs their home activities with sharp commands and then sends them out to play in the neighborhood. The husband spends almost no time with them. Both parents shout and slap when discipline is needed. Mr. Z. will often ignore them until he bursts out with angry shouts, after which he will withdraw.

Mrs. Z. has been concerned about their summer activities. She has gotten the oldest boy in a Little League and sends both of them to the local playground program. She voices disappointment at being unable to pay the membership fee at the Jewish Center nearby, where the children could learn to swim.

The parents seem to favor the younger child, Danial, over the older one, Jonathan, by disciplining him less and requiring fewer tasks of him.

A.2. *Relationship Between Parents and Children*

Mr. Z. is spending more time caring for the children—bathing them in the evenings and getting Sunday morning breakfast for them. Mrs. Z. has enrolled them at the Jewish Center now that their salary can cover the expense and is happy to have them both taking swimming lessons. But essentially the parents have not altered their pattern of indifference and noncommunication, and there is still little outward show of emotional warmth. Discipline is still achieved by sudden reprimands, yells, and slaps.

Mrs. Z. is attempting to change her apparent favoring of the younger child. She is trying to be less severe in disciplining Jonathan and commending him upon the small progress he makes in school.

The older one is frequently told that "he is old enough to know better." While there is no outright rejection, the mother frequently exhibits annoyance and the father habitually displays indifference to them.

A.3. *Relationship Among Children*

The two children, Jonathan and Danial, feel strongly that they have a common origin. When his Grandmother presents him with candy, Jonathan always asks whether she brought some for Danial too. Danial follows Jonathan around on his adventures in the neighborhood and boasts that his big brother plays in the Little League. Although Jonathan attempts to "lose" his younger brother, he goes to the playground program with him in the summer and usually can tell his mother where to find the younger one.

Jonathan is jealous, however, of Danial's position as

A.3. *Relationship Among Children*

Jonathan, on the swim team, has told Danial that, when he grows a little and becomes a stronger swimmer, he can join too. He continues to bully him at home, however, refusing to share toys. But he now allows him to enter his room and has stopped making each meal a battlefield.

"baby" in the family. Danial
receives what little show of
affection there is, and
Jonathan reacts by talking
loudly, creating a disturbance at meals, refusing to
share toys with his brother
and sometimes bullying him.

A.4. *Family Solidarity*

Although they have prob-
lems, the family presents a
fairly united front. The only
weakness in family solidarity
is Mrs. Z.'s involvement of
her father in family affairs,
often leading to the exclusion
of her husband in decision
making (see also A.1.b.).
They visit in-laws (the L.'s)
many times a week; the parents bowl together twice a
month; they have meals together when schedules permit; they attempt to keep
their home and grounds in
order. Mrs. Z. entertained for
a visiting sister by inviting
the entire extended family to
her recreation room. Twice a
year they take the children
by car to visit Mr. Z.'s family
130 miles away.

A.4. *Family Solidarity*

No changes in the activity
patterns of the family, but
Mrs. Z. has been trying to
become less involved with
her family of origin and has
reduced the amount of complaining to her father about
her husband (see also A.1.b.).

The entire family usually
has Friday-night supper with
Mrs. Z.'s parents, where her
father will recite prayers and
the mother will serve traditional dishes. Lately Mrs.
L. has been unable to have
them all to dinner, and so
the children take turns
being guests. On hot days
the Z.'s and the L.'s go to
the shore together; in the au-
tumn they have picnics in the
park. On holidays the ex-
tended family meets at an
aunt's large house for a
barbecue.

There is very little out-
ward show of emotional
warmth in this family. Hugs
and kisses are reserved for
few occasions and are generally given only to the
younger boy. The grand-
parents do not kiss the
children when they arrive
and give only small pecks on
the cheek before bedtime.
When Mrs. Z.'s sister arrived
after an extended absence,
the greetings were pleasant
but did not indicate the state
of pleasure that the family
members testified that they
felt at the reunion. It may be

noted that the L. family
gives free rein to feelings of
anger and frustration but
has difficulty indicating love,
pleasure, and joy. While the
grandparents see the children often, they do not spend
time playing with them or
taking them places. After
acknowledging them for a
few minutes the adults begin
their own conversation, generally ignoring the children
for the rest of the visit. Mr.
L. will often spend an entire
Sunday afternoon talking to
his daughter while excluding
his son-in-law as well as his
own wife.

Mr. and Mrs. Z. are avid
television watchers, take a
great interest in spectator
sports, and bowl at least once
a month. Mrs. Z. is in-
terested in modern novels,
which she likes to discuss
with her father. Neither parent is involved in community
affairs or politics. Religious
observance is restricted to
the high holidays and participation in sabbath and
holiday ritual at the home of
the maternal grandparents
(see also D.1.).

B. INDIVIDUAL BEHAVIOR AND ADJUSTMENT

1. *Parents*

a. *History*

(1) *Mr. Z.'s* parents were Jewish immigrants born in Russia who first settled in New York City and later came to Delaware for purposes of making a living. Born in 1939, Mr. Z. was an only child left motherless at the age of eight. He was raised by an aunt with three children of her own while his father ran a store in a nearby town. Mr. Z. always felt unwelcome in his aunt's home; he saw his father only for brief periods on Sunday afternoons when he visited him at the store.

The aunt's home was in a middle-class neighborhood. Her husband ran a small dry-cleaning establishment; they managed on a tight budget. The aunt was active in Jewish affairs, and the children took part in Jewish-center activities, which Mr. Z. also joined. The elder Mr. Z. centered all his interest in the business and real-estate investments that he managed to make over the years.

Mr. Z. attended an eastern-seaboard state university, lived in a fraternity house, majored in dramatics. Well liked, he became something of a campus celebrity, officiating as disc jockey at many functions. On vacations he worked as short-order cook at a luncheonette. After graduation he joined the Air Force, was trained as a navigator, married his wife when he was 23, approximately a year-and-a-half before separation from service.

(2) *Mrs. Z.'s* parents, U.S. born, were also Jewish, of New Jersey origin. Both were high-school graduates. There were four daughters in the family, with Mrs. Z. being the youngest, born in 1943.

There was always a great deal of conflict in Mrs. Z.'s parental home. Mr. L. felt superior to his wife, was autocratic in manner, and showed little respect or regard for family members. The L.'s had married originally when they were just out of high school because of an unwanted pregnancy, and both extended families were suspicious and unfriendly to each other. When Mrs. Z. was born her mother worked in the family grocery, and a good deal of Mrs. Z.'s childhood was spent in the store with her mother. She was ignored by the father, who had wanted a son, and she was a bother to her overworked mother. Mrs. Z.'s older sisters took over some of her care. With the oldest she had an especially close relationship, but the younger one was always jealous of her. Her mother was always in poor health and finally gave up working when Mrs. Z. was 12. The parents often talked of separating or of obtaining a divorce. Although they did not regularly attend religious services, they celebrated major holidays and took part in Jewish-center activities. Mr. L.'s greatest concern was to make more money. Since his children were female, he did not plan to send them to college.

The family lived in a variety of apartments in lower-class neighborhoods close to their grocery, which gave a small and irregular income. Finally, they moved to a suburb and bought a store there that gave them a more secure financial footing. Their social contacts were limited to the extended family.

When the oldest sister married and moved away, the first of Mrs. Z.'s delinquent episodes occurred. She was caught stealing money and cigarettes to give to schoolboy acquaintances. She received therapy at the city Child Guidance Clinic for approximately six months. Although the therapists asked to see the parents, her father refused.

While at high school, where she did above-average academic work, she was involved in a number of love affairs. Once more in therapy, the whole family became involved, the father now becoming concerned and attempting to spend time with her and to change his attitudes.

One sister married a businessman and lives in the same community; two married professionals and have moved to other parts of the country. All of them enjoy higher standards of living than the Z. family.

Mrs. Z. attended a state college for a year before she married. Her father, attempting to undo years of neglect, paid her tuition, took her on trips, bought her a great deal of clothing. At school she took liberal-arts courses, was interested in art, became an officer in a nonresident sorority. The only job she had before marriage was as checkout girl in a supermarket. As for hobbies, she knitted well, liked to bowl, and was good in organizing club activities.

B.1.b. *Present Functioning:*

(1) *Mr. Z.* is short, stocky, dark-haired with a pleasant smile. He likes to tell jokes and humorous stories; will become extremely quiet if overlooked. He tells tall tales about his selling adventures and achievements. He has had a number of accidents lately while selling and he enjoys telling of them in detail, dwelling on physical symptoms. He is interested in work, sports, latest sports statistics. A college graduate, he cannot discuss books or problems of the day with his professional relatives, who believe he has no aptitude for abstract thinking.

B.1.b. *Present Functioning:*

(1) [Mr. Z.] There have been no accidents lately and there is no dwelling on hardluck stories in his conversation.

Mr. Z. enjoys a good social relationship with customers to the liquor store. He talks easily and familiarly with them and they ask for him if Mr. L. happens to be there.

Mr. Z. was very upset when his mistake led to the closing of the store for two weeks. He was depressed once more during that period but recovered soon after the store re-opened.

He boasts about his influence in managing the estab-

Mr. Z. finds it difficult to work without outside direction and authority and becomes unable to move when things seem to be going badly. He feels himself unsuccessful in providing for his family and bristles at any imagined insult. He very openly relies upon his father-in-law's advice. Outwardly he does not seem perturbed by the amount of authority his wife has assumed in the marriage. He has exhibited no open resentment about his wife's close relationship to her father.

He seems to feel he was born to bad luck and gets pleasure in recounting examples of it. He is anxious about his selling job. Presently he is trying hard to win a sales contest. There is some animosity with a district manager who was once his wife's boyfriend. He gets advice from his wife on how to handle this man. He also takes her advice on how to approach other management individuals and how to recruit junior salesmen.

lishment, although Mr. L. does not allow him to make major decisions. He seems to be happy with the position and is no longer anxious about his ability to provide for his family.

He has just joined The Lions Club and has been nominated to a vice-presidency. This has given him a great deal of pleasure.

He has to date shown no animosity to his father-in-law, although he is working directly under him.

(2) *Mrs. Z.* is about thirty pounds overweight and pays little attention to her appearance. Having few clothes, she spends the day in old slacks or shorts. Her speech is rapid and can change quickly from interest to anger or animosity. She admits that she tends to "fly off the handle" easily and does not mince words. Her interests center around the neighborhood and her husband's job. She would like to be active in B'nai B'rith Women, if she could afford a sitter so she could attend afternoon meetings.

Mrs. Z. is usually well liked. Although decisive, she has a friendly manner. Quick to draw others out, she is equally quick in making up her mind and giving instructions. She shows little external love in caring for the children.

She believes that the family has more than its share of bad luck, and like her husband, wallows in descriptions of misfortune. She enters into discussions with

(2) *Mrs. Z.* has now lost weight and cut her hair, although she does not frequent beauty parlors but fixes it at home. With a better income she has augmented her wardrobe, although she still wears slacks for her daily work.

Unlike her husband, she still indulges in hard-luck stories, recounting the latest illness of the children or the latest difficulty at work or school.

She now hires a sitter so that she can play mah jongg, thus freeing her mother, and also so she can attend B'nai B'rith Women's meetings, where she has been elected corresponding secretary.

The days of depression seem to have gone. She now exhibits much energy in keeping the house orderly, and she now has new furniture in which she takes great pride.

She is attempting to spend less time with her father. They have limited visits to one a week. Her attitude toward her mother remains unchanged.

relatives, who believe she is of above-average intelligence. She is usually preoccupied with problems related to money, insurance, illness, or her husband's job.

Mrs. Z. also has fits of depression and exhibits great lassitude at times. Whole days will elapse when she will sit by a card table putting puzzles together. She pulls herself together enough to direct the children, do necessary chores, make meals and shop. The house, however, is not tidy and her mother often comes in to clean up.

As a neighbor, she is constantly involved in swapping favors and spends a good deal of her time talking with neighbors.

She is not happy with her passive husband and looks forward to the companionship of her father. Although she helps drive her mother to required appointments, the older woman's disabilities and tendency to become wordy annoy her, and she finds it most trying to bear her. She will often dismiss

her mother in much the
same way her father has
often done, saying, "Oh, her."
or, "You know what she's
like."

(3) *Jonathan,* 9, is tall
and husky for his age, dark
skinned and curly haired. He
cannot sit still long, is very
interested in sports. He likes
saving money and has begun
a bank account. Although he
appears to be of average intelligence, and this is borne
out by psychological testing,
he is slow in learning to read
and avoids books. School is
painful and he has many
fights with children, both on
the playground and in the
classroom. When at home he
is always outside, riding his
bike and roaming the
neighborhood. Other children
describe him as belligerent
and difficult to get along
with.

Through the prodding of
his grandmother, a hearing
test was arranged for him. It
was found that he suffered
from a large loss of hearing
in one ear. At this writing,

(3) *Jonathan* has become
quieter in school and has
made progress in his work
since his ear operation. Although he still does not read
at grade level, he is no
longer required to join a special reading group from a
lower grade. His teacher also
believes he has displayed
less belligerent behavior on
the playground.

The match lighting inci-
dents have disappeared.

they are preparing to hos-
pitalize him for repair.

His problems extend from
the peer group into the
home. He has been found
lighting matches in closets.
His mother is attempting to
handle this by allowing him
to light matches under her
supervision.

(4) *Danial* is 7, blond and
short for his age. Perhaps
this is why the grandparents
still consider him the baby.
He is less active than his
brother, has a longer span of
attention, is learning at
school at a normal rate. He
gets along well with
neighborhood children and is
often invited to parties,
swimming pools, etc. He
idolizes his brother and,
whenever possible, follows
after him in play.

(4) [Danial] No change.

C. CARE AND TRAINING OF CHILDREN

1. *Physical Care*

1. *Physical Care*

Children are well
nourished, clean, adequately

No change.

clothed. Jonathan is receiving injections for an allergy. They use a doctor whenever there are signs of illness. Jonathan will soon be hospitalized for repair of his ear.

C.2. *Training Methods and Emotional Care*

There is little overt loving in this family, and praise is seldom used as an incentive. The father remains aloof; the mother often exhibits annoyance. The children roam the neighborhood with little supervision.

With few rules regulating their behavior, the boys— especially Jonathan—seem to be uncertain about what is expected of them. They are often in trouble, fighting with others on the block. For control, the mother or father will grab a child and administer a few hard slaps. There is little carry-over in setting down rules of behavior, however. The parents do not supervise play behavior or playmates. The boys are never sure when

C.2. *Training Methods and Emotional Care*

Mrs. Z. is attempting to use praise more often with the children, and encouraged by the social worker, she has given Jonathan more attention by helping him with homework and extending some supervision to his play activity.

they will be punished or
what behavior is acceptable.

Mrs. Z. is concerned about
Jonathan's episodes with
fire. Instead of physically
punishing him, she is en-
couraging him to light
matches while she watches,
and she has explained to him
why such behavior is
dangerous.

The parents, upset about
Jonathan's school behavior,
have tried to impress upon
him the importance of listen-
ing to the teacher and being
friendly with schoolmates.
But this plus teacher conferences have so far made no
difference in the situation.

D. SOCIAL ACTIVITIES

1. *Informal Associa-
tions*

The Z.'s meet with the L.'s,
Mrs. Z.'s family, with the
great-grandmother, with sisters, etc., at least once a
week. They drive down to see
Mr. Z.'s parents at Christmas
and Easter. Holidays are

1. *Informal Associa-
tions*

Mrs. Z. is attempting to
cut down on her contacts
with family of origin. She
has had peers to dinner and
is planning a party for her
sewing club. The rest is unchanged.

spent with the extended family. Mrs. Z. is friendly with her neighbors and had a neighborhood New Year's Eve party with six couples.

While they always think of themselves as members of the neighborhood, they do not belong to a neighborhood organization. They used the branch of the public library this year. They discussed recent city changes in traffic patterns and store locations with their sister on her recent trip home. They actively follow the exploits of their community's high-school football and basketball teams. However, they take little interest in political contests and do not discuss the social problems of their community.

The children's standards of behavior are haphazard, inconsistent. They have been taught, however, that there are certain ways of acting when they visit their grandmothers and they adhere to these limits.

Free time is spent watching television, talking with relatives or neighbors, seeing

a baseball game. Last year
Mr. Z. worked in his basement in the evenings, finishing it off.

D.2. *Formal Associations*

The Z.'s bowl once a month
with the company. Mrs. Z.
occasionally attends a B'nai
B'rith Women's meeting. The
oldest boy plays in Little
League and the two boys use
the summer playground program.

The Z.'s are not members
of a synagogue or the Jewish
center because they cannot
afford the fees. Jonathan attends a Temple Hebrew
school three times a week to
learn Jewish history and the
Hebrew language. The ma-
ternal grandparents, who are
members of this temple, pay
his tuition.

D.2. *Formal Associations*

The Z.'s no longer regu-
larly bowl. Mrs. Z. attends
B'nai B'rith Women and is
an officer. Her husband attends The Lions, and also is
an officer. Besides Little
League, the two boys now
take swimming lessons at
the Jewish center, an in-
stitution close to their home.

They are now members of
a synagogue. Jonathan continues to get lessons at the
Hebrew school.

E. ECONOMIC PRACTICES

1. *Source(s) and
Amount of Income*

Mr. Z., employed by a na-
tional cookware firm, earns

1. *Source(s) and
Amount of Family Income*

Mr. Z. is now employed by
his father-in-law at a liquor

approximately $7,500 a year (in 1968) with commissions. Neither life insurance nor health insurance is provided by the firm. Mr. Z. carries his G.I. insurance and has a private health-insurance policy with a high premium. Mrs. Z. finds it difficult to live within the income since it fluctuates from week to week. She food shops carefully and seldom buys herself clothing. Much of the boys' clothing is handed down from Mrs. Z.'s sister's sons. Her father buys the boys their heavy outerwear each winter. Mr. Z. will buy a suit on sale when necessary.

Mrs. Z. bought inexpensive carpeting for their small home, and—although she is unhappy about its appearance and wear—they are making installment payments on it and also on a second car, which they recently acquired. Their living-room sofa, bedroom set, boys' beds are all contributions from the extended family. They continue to eat on a card table and chairs bought in their first year of marriage.

Mrs. Z. is very bitter be-

store in an outlying suburb, earning $13,000 a year. He still carries his former life-insurance and health policies.

Mrs. Z. has bought herself a number of new outfits and a new coat. Mr. Z. has supplemented his sport wardrobe. Mrs. Z. has bought new furniture for the living/dining-room area. They are now members of the Jewish center, and they went on a vacation trip this summer.

Mrs. Z. continues to be a careful shopper and the pattern of dressing the boys in hand-me-downs continues.

cause they have never taken a vacation. When Mr. Z. takes a few days off during the year they drive down to see his parents. She is very envious of her sisters and other family members who manage annual trips. She is also envious of other members who maintain Center memberships and send children to camp. Although the family cannot be considered deprived—food, shelter, and a minimum of clothing is provided—it is straining to maintain itself on the present income level.

E.2. *Job Situation*

Mr. Z. is a salesman for a cookware firm that is decentralized, though national, and that expects him to spend some of his time without remuneration enlisting and training new applicants. He must buy his samples and the free wares he leaves at each door from the company and is required to eat lunch at a restaurant twice a week with other area salesmen—all these expenses

E.2. *Job Situation*

Mr. Z., now working for his father-in-law, has a schedule of hours, responsibilities, and pay that makes him happier. In the beginning he began to make decisions about buying and selling that his father-in-law later countermanded. He now acts strictly as a clerk, and although he has grumbled to his wife about this, he has accepted it more or less gracefully.

substantially reduce his take-home pay.

He seems to get along well with co-workers, but his district manager is an old beau of his wife's and he feels insecure and inferior working under him. He is essentially dissatisfied with the job, although he is afraid that this feeling testifies to his inadequacies. From time to time he tries to apply for other jobs, but he does so in a half-hearted manner and finds—or says he finds—it very difficult to take the time off for interviews.

He has been working for this firm six years and his wife is accustomed to his hours. She helps him a great deal keeping accounts, filling orders, answering the telephone about training new salesmen, but she is often angry about giving so much extra time. Still she prefers the security of this position to the insecurity they experienced when he was trying to sell insurance. The children, largely unaffected by their father's job, are perhaps inconvenienced at certain times when the filling of or-

He was very morose after the run-in with the police, when the liquor license was temporarily revoked. His father-in-law rebuked him very sharply, and there was a recurrence of debilitating depression. When the store reopened this disappeared. He brags to outsiders that he is the boss, but his wife, who knows better, remains quietly loyal.

There are continuing crises that try the father-in-law's patience and short temper. But until now the situation has remained satisfactory.

ders makes them stay out of
the recreation room.

E.3. *Use of Money*

Mr. Z. seems to be very
happy with the present arrangement concerning the
management of his salary.
His wife not only pays bills
and doles out allowances but
also makes the decisions
about when to buy what. She
consults her father on matters of insurance and interest
and used his advice in buying their home. They have
no savings. Mr. Z. has G.I.
insurance and a private
medical-insurance policy.
Two items that Mrs. Z.
bought upon purchasing
their home were considered
extravagant by her
parents—custom-made
drapes and wall-to-wall carpeting. Her husband, how-
ever, concurred with her decision. The second car might
also be termed an extrava-
gance, but both the Z.'s insist
that she needs transportation
during the day while he
needs the car for work. Thus,

E.3. *Use of Money*

Mrs. Z. continues to make
decisions about the allocation
of money. Under Mr. L.'s
prodding, they have started a
small savings account. Mrs.
Z. bought new furniture for
their home. They have
finished paying for the garage and carpeting, and their
debts now include payments
on the car and on the new
furniture. Mrs. Z. now admits that she enjoys making
decisions about spending
money.

their debts now include
payments for the carpeting
and the new car. They also
owe money on a garage. The
builder for the garage they
contracted filed bankruptcy
halfway through construction
and then disappeared. They
could not recover the money
that they had prepaid, and,
because of a clause in the
contract, they also found
themselves liable to the bank
for the entire amount. Thus,
they were required by law to
pay twice for an uncompleted
structure. Although they
consulted Mr. L.'s lawyer,
they found they had no
choice but to make payments
to the bank (see also E.1.).

F.   HOME AND HOUSEHOLD PRACTICES

1.   *Physical Facilities*

The Z.'s own their home, a
three-bedroom ranch in a development of ninety homes
that was built about six
years ago. The rooms are
small but the kitchen is
large enough for the family

1.   *Physical Facilities*

The Z.'s live in the same
home. The recreation room is
now habitable but the children still use the living room
for play. The garage is still
half finished.

Old dilapidated furnish-

to take their meals there.
Each boy has a room of his
own. There is one small
bathroom, which seems sufficient for the size and age of
the family. The basement
has been converted into a
recreation room, but a good
part of it is filled with boxes
of materials for orders. The
Z.'s have painted the house
once since they moved in.
The grounds are kept in relatively good condition, and a
half-finished garage is in the
deep backyard, which also
has a swing set (a present
from a sister) and old lawn
furniture.

The neighborhood is resi-
dential, an outlying section
of a medium-sized New Jersey community. The homes
are all the same age and
type. There is little traffic on
the street. Children play on
the lawns and in the back-
yards; the school and
Jewish center are just three
and four blocks away.

The Z.'s own a large re-
frigerator, washer, and
dryer, all bought when they
were first married. The
living-room sofa was given
ings have been replaced.
There is new furniture in the
living room—sofa, chairs,
tables—and a dinette set in
the kitchen.

them by Mrs. L.; they have a television set and card-table upon which they eat. Their bedroom set was sent by Mr. Z.'s parents, and the boys' beds and chests came from miscellaneous relatives.

F.2. *Housekeeping Standards*

Inside, the home is rather neglected. The children play in the living room rather than the basement, and the litter is seldom picked up. Garbage sits in paper bags in the kitchen. The counterspace is limited in the kitchen and always overflowing with food, notes, etc. The beds are left unmade and dust is not vacuumed. There is little attempt to keep the home attractive, although the tasteful color scheme, carpeting, and drapes testify to the fact that at one time this must have been important to Mrs. Z.

Household chores are carried out by Mrs. Z. The cleaning and straightening,

F.2. *Houskeeping Standards*

Chores are still apportioned in the same way. The inside of the house is kept cleaner. The garbage is no longer standing in the kitchen. Mrs. Z. attempts to keep the living room cleaner, but the boys' rooms are still in disarray.

Mrs. Z. continues to shop carefully, using food ads when possible. Meals are the same, but more expensive cuts of meat occasionally appear.

Clothing is apportioned similarly, with the exception of Mrs. Z.'s wardrobe. She has bought both sport and dress clothing, with a sister as an adviser. Her buying has remained in the moder-

when done, are her responsibilities, as are the dishes,
the cooking, and the laundry.
The boys are supposed to
make their own beds in the
morning but this is often
forgotten or done poorly. Mr.
Z. empties the garbage at
night and is supposed to
clean up in the recreation
room every week after orders
are filled, but these tasks are
most often neglected.

Meals are served on a regular schedule, with the most
substantial meal in the eve-
ning, when all are home.
Mrs. Z. knows a great deal
about nutrition, buys wisely,
and serves a variety of dishes, many of them never
made in her own childhood
home. There is a great deal
of snacking, and con-
sequently the boys eat little
at their regular meals. Mrs.
Z. seldom prohibits their
foraging for food between
meals since she herself is a
nibbler. Both she and her
husband enjoy eating and
cooking, and he often helps
cook on weekends. Some of
the new dishes are from his
repertoire. Whenever

ate price range, although she
has been encouraged to
spend more by her wealthier
sister. Mr. Z. has bought
slacks and sport shirts to
wear in the liquor store.

The Z.'s bought new furniture for the living room, din-
ing room, and kitchen. Mrs.
Z. would like to replace the
draperies and carpeting too,
but wistfully adds she knows
it cannot be done at this
time.

They took their first vacation this summer, renting a
camper and traveling to
state parks.

possible he barbecues on
Sunday.

The major portion of their
weekly income goes for food.
Mrs. Z. shops for groceries at
a discount store quite a distance from their home where
slightly damaged canned
goods or mangled chickens
can be gotten for less. They
try to use hand-me-downs for
the children but buy all
shoes at reputable shoe
stores. Outer clothing is do-
nated by Mr. L. Mr. Z. buys
a suit on sale every three or
four years. Mrs. Z. buys little
clothing. They recently acquired a second car, used. No
furniture purchases have
been made in the past six
years. Materials for the
finishing of the basement
were bought last year and
they are making payments
on the ill-fated garage. They
take no trips or vacations,
although they drive down to
see Mrs. Z.'s parents once a
year. They do not often hire
sitters. They have an individual health-insurance plan
and pay for drugs and doctor's visits at each health
emergency.

G. HEALTH CONDITIONS AND PRACTICES

1. *Health Conditions*

Mr. Z. has injuries from two accidents that occurred during the past year: in the first instance he fell into a hole near a new building while making his selling rounds, and in the second, he was struck from behind by another vehicle while waiting to make a turn in his car. His arm, shoulder, and back give him pain. He has been going to a private doctor for almost a year and wears a back brace. Although the car claim was settled, the other claim he filed for negligence is still outstanding, since neither the contractor nor the house owner wishes to accept responsibility. The soreness of his back and arm make it difficult for him to carry his sample case.

Mrs. Z. is in good physical condition. Whenever the children have colds, however, she is prone to catch them, remaining ill for three or more weeks, during which

1. *Health Conditions*

Mr. Z.'s back no longer bothers him, although he sometimes suffers pain when moving heavy cases in the liquor store.

Mrs. Z. is in good health; she still suffers colds.

Jonathan had ear surgery, and the operation was termed successful. He is doing better work in school.

time she finds it impossible to carry on with household tasks.

Jonathan has a hearing defect that has just been detected. Other than that, he seems normal. Testing in school and at agency has revealed no learning disability despite his school difficulties.

Danial wears glasses for a slight cross-eyed condition. Otherwise healthy.

G.2. *Health Practices*

The family obtains medical care from private physicians whenever necessary. They follow the medical advice given them and buy prescribed medications.

They follow middle-class hygiene practices as far as food preparation, dishwashing, personal cleanliness are concerned.

They do not have regular dental checkups (Mrs. Z. cannot justify the expense) but use a dentist when necessary. Mrs. Z. and Danial had dental work this year. Neither adults nor children make a practice of

G.2. *Health Practices*

No change.

regularly brushing their
teeth.

H. RELATIONSHIP TO INTERVENTION WORKER

1. *Attitude Toward Worker*

Mrs. Z. made inquiries, contacted the agency on her own. She is very cooperative, sincerely wishes to describe accurately the home situation and gain help from worker. After two visits, though, she expressed some doubt about the worker's ability to help. Mr. Z. insisted they had no problems and refused to come to either interview. Mrs. Z. is seen twice a month, while Jonathan is seeing a psychologist and is undergoing psychometric testing.

1. *Attitude Toward Worker*

Mrs. Z., who attends monthly sessions, is grateful to the worker for the changes that have been made in her relationship and for her better understanding of herself and the family situation. However, she expresses the feeling that more of the improvements in family life were due to a change in employment than to social-work treatment. Mr. Z. attends sessions, is no longer as defensive, and exhibits some gratitude to worker. Jonathan has also been seen jointly with his parents at irregular intervals.

H.2. *Use of Worker*

Mrs. Z. is using the worker both to vent her feelings

H.2. *Use of Worker*

Mrs. Z. no longer uses the worker to vent feelings, but

about her husband and to
gain advice in the interpersonal areas of family life.
She would like to effect
change in her relationship
with Mr. Z. and thus create a
less tense home atmosphere.
Some of the second session
was devoted to describing
her feelings about her children and parents. The
worker is encouraging her to
find new ways of dealing
with her older son. Mr. Z.
has been invited to come but
has found himself "too busy"
to attend the session.

rather as a resource to give
advice and to help achieve
understanding. Mr. Z. uses
the worker as adviser but
not as a help toward understanding underlying
psychological mechanisms.

I.   USE OF COMMUNITY RESOURCES

1.   *School*

Both parents want their
children to be successful in
school. They have expressed
a desire to have them go
through college, although at
the moment they do not
know how they could man-
age it financially. They insist
the children attend regu-
larly, be on time, do

1.   *School*

Jonathan is reading better
since his ear operation and is
less aggressive. He is continuing in Hebrew school because of his improved
functioning and is generally
on a par with the others in
his class. Mrs. Z.' has become
an active member of the
elementary school P.T.A. and

homework. Mrs. Z. attends when the children are in special programs. She has had conferences with Jonathan's teachers during which his reading difficulties and aggression have been discussed. She contacted the school nurse about Jonathan's hearing difficulties before a private physician was consulted. The nurse gave him preliminary testing and then suggested they see a physician.

Jonathan uses any excuse to stay away from school. He does not do the extra homework that was given him to improve his reading. In fact, attempts to make him do the work at home created so much trouble (crying, anger) that Mrs. Z. has given up trying to work with him after school.

He also attends Hebrew classes two days a week after school and each Sunday morning. They have received reports of trouble from his teacher also and are thinking of letting him drop these classes altogether, since his difficulties seem to increase the parent's association of the Hebrew school.

on those days when he is expected to sit still for long
periods of time.

Danial, on the other hand,
has proved cooperative and
successful in school. He has
not yet started Hebrew
school.

I.2. *Religious Institutions*

The family is not a
member of a congregation
because they cannot afford
the membership fee. They attend High Holy Day services
at the parents' synagogue
(tickets for these services are
sold separately), sharing
three seats among the four of
them. A few times a year on
special holidays they attend
services at the L.'s
synagogue, bringing the boys
with them for purposes of introducing the boys to the
holiday and the ritual. As
noted, Jonathan attends a
Hebrew school affiliated with
the grandparents' synagogue.
The Z.'s feel it is important
to transmit culture and religion to their children and

I.2. *Religious Institutions*

The family has joined the
parents' synagogue and pay
$150 dues a year. They at-
tend services on an average
of ten times a year. Mrs. Z.
has become an active
member of the Sisterhood.

feel strongly about attendance at such a school.

I.3. *Health Resources*

The Z.'s use private doctors
and dentists, patronize private pharmacies. The use of
the school nurse for hearing
tests is unusual for they
usually use private
facilities.

I.3. *Health Resources*

No change.

I.4. *Social Agencies*

Mrs. Z. cooperates with the
local Family Service Agency
and believes they will help
her marriage. She feels they
helped her in the past and
will do so in the present. Mr.
Z. is resentful, defensive,
ashamed to be connected
with the agency.
They do not make use of
other agencies.

I.4. *Social Agencies*

Mr. Z. exhibits less defensive and shamed behavior
but has mentioned that they
can now terminate agency
help since they seem to be
doing better.

I.5. *Recreational Agencies*

The Z.'s use the summer
playground program and li-

I.5. *Recreational Agencies*

They now use the Jewish
center facilities as paying

brary for their children.
Jonathan plays in Little
League. They do not use Boy
Scout or similar programs.

The Z.'s use town parks,
swimming lakes, and state
shore facilities. They cannot
afford the Jewish center
facilities or private pools.
They have never tried the
"Y," which is situated a long
distance from their house.

members. Otherwise no
change.

On the following pages ratings on the social functioning of
the Z. family, separated as to beginning and after situations,
are presented. The rating was done by three independent individuals, all of whom had previous experience in this type of
coding. On all main categories and all subcategories but one
(health conditions) the three raters either agreed on scores
(50.7%) or two agreed while the third checked the adjacent
position (49.3%). (There was a difference of opinion about the
seriousness of the health problems in the beginning situation;
one rater coded them as marginal while the other two
evaluated them as near adequate.) Where coders disagreed as
described above, the scores that are shown represent the majority view, that is, the concurrence of two coders. On health
conditions, a near-adequate rating was agreed upon at a conference of the three. Score sheets for beginning and after situations and for movement, with a graphic movement Profile as
well, follow the discussion of the ratings.

RATIONALE FOR SCORE ASSIGNED

Subcategory   *Beg.*   *After*

Marital Rela-
tionship   5   Conflict for this couple
                                      revolves around unfulfilled
                                      aspirations and needs—
                                      wealth and social position.
                                      The husband is unable to
                                      measure up to expectations.
                                      A rating of *4* would be too
                                      low, since both spouses ex-
                                      press concern for the rela-
                                      tionship and a need to
                                      maintain the partnership,
                                      even though the wife does
                                      not respect the husband's
                                      position in the family.
                                      Routineness seems more
                                      the pattern than pleasure
                                      in the relationship. Lack
                                      of communication and
                                      inability to talk through
                                      their feelings pervade the
                                      situation. Hence a rating
                                      of *5*—above marginal
                                      rather than *6*—near ade-
                                      quate.
                        6   Despite some continued
                                      reticence about open discus-
                                      sion, there is considerably

Subcategory:	Beg.	After

| Marital Rela-tionship (continued) | | more pleasure derived from this marriage than earlier. Each partner can perform his/her tasks more confidently, though Mr. Z. had some problems in this new job. |

Subcategory:

| Parent-Child Relationship | 5 | Since consistency of treatment and impartiality are not strong points in this family, the rating hovers around marginal. The mother reacts erratically, and the father is indifferent until he explodes. The partiality shown to the young child is clearly not desirable. |
| | 6 | Many of the conditions remain the same—inability to show affection, indifference, erratic and inconsistent discipline. But the conscious effort to relate, to treat the children more equally, and the awareness of the need to create a new climate enables us to rate |

Subcategory: *Beg.*   *After*

Parent-Child
Relationship   this household near
(continued)   adequate.

Sibling Rela-
tionship   7   Determining how much
                                            "sibling rivalry" is accepta-
                                            ble within a family is dif-
                                            ficult, and while we do not
                                            wish to perpetuate the
                                            "boys will be boys " theory,
                                            it is evident that the
                                            younger child admires his
                                            brother and that the older,
                                            though somewhat jealous,
                                            cares for his little brother.
                                            We cannot expect all pos-
                                            sessions to be shared or all
                                            of their time to be spent to-
                                            gether.
                                                There is nothing here to
                                            suggest an atypical problem
                                            or severe conflict, and since
                                            there are many positives,
                                            we consider this
                                            7—adequate.
                           7   The basic attitudes and
                                            behavior remain the same.

Subcategory:

Family Solidar-
ity   6   Clearly, the near-

Subcategory: *Beg.*   *After*

Family Solidar-
ity   marginal 5 or less is not
(continued)   applicable because the Z.'s
                           are a solidary family, but
                           some soul searching is re-
                           quired to make the distinc-
                           tion between 6 and 7. This
                           family obviously operates
                           as a cohesive unit—they eat
                           together, spend leisure time
                           together; certainly their
                           goals are consistent with
                           community standards. Even
                           the wife's dependence upon
                           her own father, while in
                           some circumstances unde-
                           sirable, does not diminish
                           the rating, since the hus-
                           band does not seem to re-
                           sent it.
                               Here, the missing link is
                           "satisfaction," "warmth and
                           affection" derived from the
                           togetherness, preventing an
                           outright 7.
                   7   While much of the be-
                           havior is the same, the
                           whole atmosphere in the
                           family is marked by greater
                           satisfaction. Individuals are
                           making conscious efforts to
                           improve the emotional feel-
                           ing.

	Beg.	*After*	
Main Category:			

FAMILY RE-
LATIONSHIP
AND UNITY   5   Greatest weight is
placed on the relation-
ship involving Mr. and
Mrs. Z., which dominates
the family picture. This
rating also reflects the
general shortcomings in
the parent-child relationships.
                              6   An overall rating of *6*
indicates a near-adequate
marital relationship in
the after situation and a
parent-child
relationship—also rated
6—that is guided by
some awareness of prob-
lems and efforts to over-
come them.

Subcategory:

Father   5   Law violations do not
enter this picture. Mr. Z.
gets along with people, but
he often becomes depressed,
his self-image is poor (he
dwells on hard luck), and
he tends to become im-

Subcategory: *Beg.*   *After*

| Father (continued) | | mobilized under stress. Regarding various areas of role performance, the rating is below adequate. He respects his spouse but is in conflict with her; he cares for his children but withdraws from a positive parental role, overemphasizing punishment or keeping aloof. Not strong as a breadwinner, he does work and cares about his performance in this role. Weighing the relative strengths and weaknesses, Mr. Z. falls most appropriately into 5. |
| | 6 | Mr. Z.'s new job has reinforced some character positives—i.e., the ability to get along with people. The improvement in earning capacity has given him additional confidence, warranting a higher rating. |

Subcategory:

| Mother | 5 | Mrs. Z.'s poor appearance and her complaining attest to her poor self-image. Obviously unhappy with her social position and the lack |

Subcategory: *Beg.*   *After*

Mother
(continued)

of extra income, she is still
functioning above the marginal (*4*) level, since her
behavior does not represent
a potential threat to the
welfare of the family. There
are disagreements and conflicts and hostility toward
Mr. Z., but she, nonethe-
less, helps him with his
work, responds to need.

Display of affection is
limited, and favoritism toward one child might indicate a marginal rating, yet
physical care is adequate
and her interest and con-
cern are not questioned.

She is well liked, gre-
garious, but dissatisfied
with her limited participation in outside groups. Generally, satisfaction in the
homemaking role is so limited that a rating of *5* is
indicated.

7   There is so much change
in Mrs. Z.'s appearance
(weight loss, additional clothing), role performance
(club participation, housekeeping), mental state
(fewer depressions, added

Subcategory:	*Beg.*	*After*

Mother
(continued)
Subcategory:

energy), that the jump to 7 is warranted.

Children   5

Jonathan, the older child, seems to fit the marginal description: acting-out behavior, receiving treatment for possible emotional disorder, school performance below capacity, physical handicap necessitating treatment, less-than-adequate relationship with parents, and poor attitudes toward school. Although he "lights matches," the behavior is not clearly delinquent, but by the criteria applied here it does not exceed the marginal level.

Danial, however, so fits into the adequate area that we set a 5 for the combined rating.

6   Jonathan has made considerable progress—he has been treated for his hearing problem, he is less belligerent, more conforming to norms. With Danial's functioning remaining at the adequate level, we de-

Subcategory: *Beg.*   *After*

Children   cide on a combined rating
(continued)   of 6 rather than 7, for
                                      Jonathan continues to have
                                      problems at school.

Main Category:

INDIVIDUAL			
BEHAVIOR	5		This is the mean and modal rating for all family members.
		6	This rating represents the predominate rating of Individual Behavior and Adjustment in the after situation.

Subcategory:

Physical Care   7   Everything herein fits the
                                      adequate description.
                   7   Same as before.

Subcategory:

Training
Methods and
Emotional Care   5   The parents being incon-
                                      sistent, clearly showing fa-
                                      voritism to the younger
                                      child, not defining limits of
                                      acceptable behavior would

Subcategory: *Beg.*   *After*

Training
Methods and
Emotional Care
(continued)   generally fit into the mar-
                                 ginal description.
                                    But because there is posi-
                                 tive feeling, there is con-
                                 cern for the children, and
                                 there is no deviancy from
                                 community norms, we con-
                                 sider *4* too low and *5* more
                                 appropriate.
                        6   Attempts are being made
                                 by the parents to reinforce
                                 good behavior, give praise,
                                 and to show attention to
                                 Jonathan, thereby di-
                                 minishing the "favoritism"
                                 accusation.

Main Category:

CARE AND
TRAINING OF
CHILDREN   *5*   Clearly training
                                 methods carry most
                                 weight in giving a cate-
                                 gory score.
                        6   Near-adequate
                                 functioning is evident as
                                 parents make concerted
                                 effort to remedy deficien-
                                 cies in child rearing.

Subcategory:	Beg.	After	
Informal Associations	7		Consistent with "adequate" description. Relationships with family and friends are good; both Mr. and Mrs. Z. are friendly and well liked; and there is general agreement on leisure-time activities between the two.
		7	Same as before.

Subcategory:			
Formal Associations	6		Although there is a positive attitude toward organizations to which they belong, there is frustration over their inability to join the Jewish center, suggesting that a 6 rather than a 7 rating is most appropriate.
		7	The family is now in a position to make good use of formal organizations.

Main Category:			
SOCIAL ACTIVITIES	7		Social activities are preponderately adequate.
		7	No change from the before situation.

Subcategory:	Beg.	After

Source and
Amount of In-
come   5

　　　　　　　　　　Although family is dis-
　　　　　　　　　　satisfied with marginal,
　　　　　　　　　　somewhat irregular, in-
　　　　　　　　　　come, Mr. Z. is working
　　　　　　　　　　regularly and needs are
　　　　　　　　　　met, even if there are no
　　　　　　　　　　extras.

　　　　　　7　　　There is a substantial
　　　　　　　　　　improvement in this situa-
　　　　　　　　　　tion. Income has increased,
　　　　　　　　　　allowing for some extras,
　　　　　　　　　　and the family enjoys more
　　　　　　　　　　security.

Subcategory:

Job Situation   5

　　　　　　　　　　Mr. Z.'s work pattern is
　　　　　　　　　　steady, although it is ap-
　　　　　　　　　　parent he is dissatisfied
　　　　　　　　　　with the job and frustrated
　　　　　　　　　　over his inability to get a
　　　　　　　　　　better position.

　　　　　　7　　　Mr. Z. is obviously more
　　　　　　　　　　suited to his new role and
　　　　　　　　　　pleased with the situation.

Subcategory:

Use of Money   6

　　　　　　　　　　Despite some bad debts,
　　　　　　　　　　management of money and
　　　　　　　　　　payment of the debts is
　　　　　　　　　　planned. The major dissen-
　　　　　　　　　　sion is in the wife's resent-

Subcategory: *Beg.*   *After*

Use of Money   ment of her role as man-
(continued)   ager.

              7   Now that Mrs. Z. has not
                       only adjusted to but ac-
                       knowledged her liking for
                       the responsibility of money
                       manager, the rating has
                       risen to 7.

Main Category:

ECONOMIC
PRACTICES   5   The prevailing feeling
                       of dissatisfaction in each
                       area puts the overall
                       rating at 5, or above
                       marginal.

              7   An overall after rating
                       of 7 is identical with
                       each subcategory rating
                       and reflects the basically
                       positive outlook in this
                       area.

Subcategory:

Physical
Facilities   6   The neighborhood in
                       which the Z.'s live is pleas-
                       ant, and though the home
                       is small, each child has his
                       own room. The main qual-
                       ifying factors are the

Subcategory:	Beg.	After

Physical
Facilities
(continued)

"takeover" of the basement by the merchandise samples, an arrangement limiting the boys' play area and contributing to the dissatisfaction of Mrs. Z.

7   With the removal of the samples the family can better utilize the basement space.

Subcategory:

Housekeeping
Standards   6

Although the home may be in some disorder, it is far from hazardous to the welfare of the children. Meals are adequate and certainly hygiene standards are satisfactory.

7   Improvement in housekeeping standards is another indication of positive changes this family has been experiencing.

Main Category:

HOME AND
HOUSEHOLD
PRACTICES   6

The main category rating of 6 corresponds to the subcategory ratings.

Main Category: *Beg.*   *After*

| HOME AND HOUSEHOLD PRACTICES (continued) | 7 | Rating is the same as the subcategory ratings. |

Subcategory:

Health Condi-
tions   6   Back problems and some
                                        weaknesses in carrying
                                        sample cases are noted, but
                                        they do not interfere se-
                                        riously with Mr. Z.'s ability
                                        to earn a living. Nor can
                                        Mrs. Z.'s frequent colds be
                                        said to limit her function-
                                        ing.
                                        Jonathan's hearing loss is
                                        being investigated, al-
                                        though its effect upon his
                                        poor school performance is
                                        conjectural.
                   7   No major health problems
                                        are noted in the after situa-
                                        tion.

Subcategory:

Health Practices   7   Both general hygiene and
                                        attention to health are
                                        adequate, as is the Z.'s pur-
                                        suit of proper medical re-
                                        sources.

Subcategory: *Beg.*   *After*

| Health Practices (continued) | 7 | The same high standards prevail. |

Main Category:

| HEALTH CON-DITIONS AND PRACTICES | 6 | This rating takes into account the health problems that exist at this time. |
| | 7 | Overall functioning is adequate with regard to health situation and practices. |

Subcategory:

| Attitude Toward Worker | 6 | Mr. Z.'s resistance to treatment is overshadowed by the response of the rest of the family. |
| | 7 | With the father's reluctance overcome, the family reveals a basically favorable attitude toward professional services. |

Subcategory:

| Use of Worker | 6 | Mr. Z.'s resistance does not permit optimum use of the worker. |

Subcategory: *Beg.*   *After*

Use of Worker   7   Positive use of the worker
(continued)   by both parents justifies
                                     this rating.

Main Category:

RELATIONSHIP
TO WORKER   6   The before rating of
                                    the main category is in
                                    line with the subcategory
                                    ratings.
                            7   The overall after
                                    rating is the same as the
                                    subcategory ratings.

Subcategory:

Schools   6   Jonathan's problems in
                                    school make this a near-
                                    adequate rather than
                                    adequate rating.
                            7   With improvement in
                                    Jonathan's school behavior,
                                    the family's use of resources
                                    may be rated 7.
Subcategory:

Religious In-
stitutions   N.A.   Occasional attendance
                                    but nonmembership dic-

Subcategory: *Beg.*   *After*

Religious In-
stitutions   tates a "not applicable"
(continued)   rating.
                         7   Membership in the
                                  synagogue and attendance
                                  at services make this a 7
                                  rating.

Subcategory:

Health Re-
sources   7   This family utilizes
                                  available medical resources.
                         7   No change.

Subcategory:

Social Agencies 6   Some problems in the re-
                                  lationship to the Family
                                  Service Agency makes this
                                  only a near-adequate
                                  rating.
                         7   School agencies are well
                                  utilized in the after situa-
                                  tion.

Subcategory:

Recreation
Agencies   7   This family makes exten-
                                  sive and good use of recre-
                                  ational resources and
                                  facilities.
                         7   Same as in the before
                                  situation.

Beg. *After*

Main Category:

USE OF COM-
MUNITY RE-
SOURCES   7

                  The positive attitude toward and the reasonably good use of most of the community's resources justify an overall rating of 7 or adequate, despite the 6 ratings in two subcategories.

             7   The positive approach to the available community resources is maintained.

PROFILE OF MOVEMENT
ON Z FAMILY

	Family Relationships	Individual Behavior	Care and Training of Children	Social Activities	Economic Practices	Home and Household Practices	Health Conditions	Relationship to Worker	Use of Community Resources
Plus 4									
Plus 3									
Plus 2									
Plus 1									
No Change									
Minus 1									
Minus 2									
Minus 3									

MAIN CATEGORIES

Joint Ratings

COMPOSITE SCORES

PROFILE OF FAMILY FUNCTIONING

Family: _____ Z _____ X _____   Case No.: _____   Scorer(s): _____

1st Profile _____
2nd Profile _____
3rd Profile _____
4th Profile _____
5th Profile _____
6th Profile _____

Three Independent Raters

	Not Known	Not App.	Category Score	Subcategory Score
FAMILY RELATIONSHIPS			5	
Marital Relationship				5
Parent-Child Relationship				5
Sibling Relationship				7
Family Solidarity				6
Relationship with Other Household Members		X		

	Not Known	Not App.	Category Score	Subcategory Score
INDIVIDUAL BEHAVIOR			5	
Father				5
Mother				5
Older Children (10 & up)		X		
Younger Children (1-9)				5
CARE AND TRAINING OF CHILDREN			5	
Physical Care				7
Training Methods				5
SOCIAL ACTIVITIES			7	
Informal Associations				7
Formal Associations				6

	Not Known	Not App.	Category Score	Subcategory Score
ECONOMIC PRACTICES			5	
Source of Income				5
Job Situation				5
Use of Money				6
HOME AND HOUSEHOLD PRACTICES			6	
Physical Facilities				6
Housekeeping Standards				6
HEALTH CONDITIONS AND PRACTICES			6	
Health Conditions				6
Health Practices				7

	Not Known	Not App.	Category Score	Subcategory Score
RELATIONSHIP TO WORKER			6	
Attitude Toward Worker				6
Use of Worker				6
USE OF COMMUNITY RESOURCES			7	
School				6
Religious Institutions		X		
Health Resources				7
Social Agencies				6
Recreational Agencies				7

COMPOSITE SCORES
PROFILE OF FAMILY FUNCTIONING

Family: ____ Z ____   Case No.: _____   Scorer(s): _____

1st Profile _____
2nd Profile ___ X ___
3rd Profile _____
4th Profile _____
5th Profile _____
6th Profile _____

	Not Known	Not App.	Three Independent Raters	
			Category Score	Subcategory Score
FAMILY RELATIONSHIPS			6	
Marital Relationship				6
Parent-Child Relationship				6
Sibling Relationship				7
Family Solidarity				7
Relationship with Other Household Members		X		

	Not Known	Not App.	Category Score	Subcategory Score
INDIVIDUAL BEHAVIOR			6	
Father				6
Mother				7
Older Children (10 & up)		X		
Younger Children (1-9)				6
CARE AND TRAINING OF CHILDREN			6	
Physical Care				7
Training Methods				6
SOCIAL ACTIVITIES			7	
Informal Associations				7
Formal Associations				7

	Not Known	Not App.	Category Score	Subcategory Score
ECONOMIC PRACTICES			7	
Source of Income				7
Job Situation				7
Use of Money				7
HOME AND HOUSEHOLD PRACTICES			7	
Physical Facilities				7
Housekeeping Standards				7
HEALTH CONDITIONS AND PRACTICES			7	
Health Problems				7
Health Practices				7

	Not Known	Not App.	Category Score	Subcategory Score
RELATIONSHIP TO WORKER			7	
Attitude Toward Worker				7
Use of Worker				7
USE OF COMMUNITY RESOURCES			7	
School				7
Religious Institutions				7
Health Resources				7
Social Agencies				7
Recreational Agencies				7

MOVEMENT SCORES
PROFILE OF FAMILY FUNCTIONING

Family: ____ Z ____ Case No.: ____   Scorer(s): ____

Change Profile	Not Known	Not App.	Three Independent Raters Category Score	Subcategory Score
FAMILY RELATIONSHIPS			+1	
Marital Relationship				+1
Parent-Child Relationship				+1
Sibling Relationship				0
Family Solidarity				+1
Relationship with Other Household Members		X*		

	Not Known	Not App.	Category Scores	Subcategory Scores
INDIVIDUAL BEHAVIOR			+1	
Father				+1
Mother				+2
Older Children (10 & up)		X*		
Younger Children (1-9)				+1
CARE AND TRAINING OF CHILDREN			+1	
Physical Care				0
Training Methods				+1
SOCIAL ACTIVITIES			0	
Informal Associations				0
Formal Associations				+1

Change Profile	Not Known	Not App.	Category Score	Subcategory Score
ECONOMIC PRACTICES			+2	
Source of Income				+2
Job Situation				+2
Use of Money				+1
HOME AND HOUSEHOLD PRACTICES			+1	
Physical Facilities				+1
Housekeeping Facilities				+1
HEALTH CONDITIONS AND PRACTICES			+1	
Health Problems				+1
Health Practices				0

Change Profile	Not Known	Not App.	Category Score	Subcategory Score
RELATIONSHIP TO WORKER			+1	
Attitude Toward Worker				+/1
Use of Worker				+1
USE OF COMMUNITY RESOURCES			0	
School				+1
Religious Institutions		X*		
Health Resources				0
Social Agencies				+1
Recreational Agencies				0

* No change rating can be assigned when either beginning or after rating or both are missing.

6. Reliability and Validity

Ever since the present scale for measuring the social functioning of families—or an earlier version of it—was developed, the problems of reliability and validity have received much attention. Before we examine these issues, a few words of caution to the researcher. When reliability tests have had positive results, they have been interpreted by the researcher as constituting a mandate for the instrument's use. This writer wishes to stress, however, the importance of continuing reliability testing in future measurement endeavors, regardless of the positive results that have been reported in the past. Test reliability, after all, is not only a measure of the quality of the instrument but also of the performance of the people administering it.

The present discussion of efforts aimed at establishing reliability and validity will be limited to just a few of the more notable attempts, allowing the reader who is interested in specifics to explore the citations in depth.

In the original manual on the measurement of family functioning two types of reliability were examined: *inter-rater reliability at coding,* which tested the consistency with which two or more raters coded the narrative Profile, and the *reliability of schedule writing,* or the degree to which different people who read the same case material conceptualize and profile the material in the same way (Geismar and Ayres 1960). The latter issue is rarely dealt with in the social-science literature, because it is generally assumed that a clear conceptual scheme furnishes a built-in reliability.

Carrying out a reliability test of Profile writing is, of course, contingent upon having a reliable technique of rating family functioning. Both types of reliability were tested with the aid of three independent raters and Profile writers, and results indicated at least a minimal measure of reliability (pp. 21–25).

The recommended procedure for reliability testing is to have three independent coders read each case and compare scores.

One method of establishing criteria of inter-rater agreement is to count the percentage of ratings where three raters agree on the same scale position, where two raters agree on the same position while one checks an adjacent position, and where each rater checks a different position. If the first two alternatives can be considered acceptable criteria for reliability, the proportion of ratings meeting these conditions may be taken as an index of reliability. Tests with data in the Neighborhood Improvement Project showed reliability percentages for rating beginning position and movement to be 87.4% and 97.4%, respectively (Geismar and Krisberg, pp. 320–321).

Another aspect of inter-rater reliability was examined in the Chemung County Research Demonstration with Dependent Multi-Problem Families. In this experimental-control study of the effects of casework intervention the scores of two different teams of raters who coded identical Profiles were compared. The principal investigator reported very similar results for the two test teams, each of which was affiliated with a different organization and worked in a different area from the other (Wallace, pp. 387–388; Brown, p. 141; and Wallace and Smith).

Although more difficult to demonstrate than reliability, validity is the ultimate criterion of a measuring instrument's utility. We shall seek to bring evidence of two types of validity for the Family Functioning Scale: *internal validity,* or the consistency with which the several items tap the same dimension, or simply hang together (Riley, p. 474) and *external validity,* or the extent to which test results coincide with other known measures of the same dimension.

The strongest evidence of internal validity was supplied by its ability to meet Guttman scale requirements when an analysis of a sample of 150 lower-class, socially disorganized families was carried out (Geismar, LaSorte, and Ayres). It was found that Profile scores for a random sample of 555 young, urban families did not meet scalability requirements, but intercorrelations among areas of social functioning were all significant above the .001 level and ranged from r's of .578 to .799

for correlations between area score and total score, and r's from .378 to .807 for intercorrelations among eight areas of social functioning (Geismar 1973, pp. 255-256). (The area Relationship to the Social Worker was not included because the research population was not receiving services.)

External validity was tested in one instance by independent interviews with husbands and wives (N=40) and a comparison of their responses on nineteen items and six dimensions of behavior and beliefs in family life. The test was based on the assumption that husband-wife agreement regarding various aspects of family functioning is evidence that their independent reports correspond to the actual situation and may, therefore, be considered valid. Agreement ratios ranged from .73 to .93, with a mean of .80 and a standard deviation of .067 (Geismar, Lagay, Wolock, Gerhart, and Fink, pp. 35-45).

A more rigorous test of external validity was provided by comparing the results of movement measured by the Family Functioning Scale with those obtained by another standardized instrument, the Community Service Society Scale, also known as the Hunt-Kogan Scale, which measures change due to social-service intervention. The occasion for this validity test was the above-mentioned Chemung County Study. Results of the measurement of outcome on the two movement scales for both experimental and control groups were very similar. A comparison of ratings for identical cases showed that "in more than 40 percent of the cases the ratings were the same, while in another 40 percent the differences were no greater than one degree" (Wallace, pp. 387-388).

7. Other Statistical Issues in
Data Analysis

As we have stated earlier, the family-functioning scale was designed to assess the social functioning of seriously disorganized families. The score continuum, which ranges from 7 to *1*, adequate to inadequate, was set up to cover all forms of behavior encountered in family research, with the marginal position of *4* considered the theoretical midpoint around which the functioning of problematic families would cluster.

Early studies with multiproblem families showed that while some areas and subcategories—particularly those representing expressive behavior—showed a reasonably normal distribution around a mean of *4* or less, other areas were skewed in the direction of better behavior. Two studies based on samples of lower-class, seriously problematic families showed overall means for nine areas of 3.85 and 4.38, respectively (Geismar and Krisberg, p. 330; Geismar and Ayres 1959, pp. 8–9). Research with less-deprived families shows higher mean scores with more skewing in the direction of adequate functioning (Geismar 1964, p. 104; Geismar 1969, pp. 19–36). Also, while samples of multiproblem families yielded score distributions that met requirements for Guttman scalability (Geismar, LaSorte and Ayres), the scores of less-problematic populations were not scalable. This variability in score characteristics, reflecting, of course, differences in functioning traits, must be taken into account when analyzing data. The following guidelines were designed to be of help in this situation.

When scores are reasonably well distributed and not unduly skewed in any area, analysis can take into account all or nearly all the score positions (given a large enough sample) and utilize parametric statistical techniques. When scores are skewed and/or the distribution has a limited spread, data can be handled most appropriately by combining score positions and employing statistical devices that are nonparametric.

An alternate technique, especially appropriate if the data prove to be nonscalable, is factor analysis. The goal here is to reduce a large number of items to sets of common factors or dimensions. Factor analysis of the Family Functioning Profile should be based on the most basic units of observation, the twenty-six subcategories rather than the nine main areas, which are likely to constitute main foci of the analysis. Our own application of the factor-analytic technique to family-functioning data yielded statistical factors that paralleled to some extent the conceptual areas (main categories) comprising the St. Paul Scale (Geismar 1973, pp. 48–53, 255–258).[8]

Another scale refinement that might be contemplated is *multiple-regression analysis,* a method that offers the opportunity to develop area weights, which can then be used to score the total social functioning of a family. It is clear that the contribution of each area to overall family functioning varies considerably, depending on such factors as family size, life-cycle stage, and social class. In our presently used method of analysis each area has been given equal weight in the total score, and the area interrelationships are examined afterwards by means of Guttman scaling or correlational analysis. In multiple-regression analysis a weighting system would be developed so that the total family scores would be based on weighted subscores, reflecting the contribution of each area to overall family functioning within a given universe of families.

8. *Including the Family in the Rating of Family Functioning*

The Scale of Family Functioning is designed to make assessments of social functioning and changes in that functioning on the basis of interview data and interviewer observa-

---

8. A subcategory factor analysis done with a sample of 555 young urban families yielded five factors composed of variables with loadings ranging from .577 to .838. The factors were tentatively identified as expressive-interpersonal relationships, instrumental functioning, economic functioning, formal associations, and health conditions. Some of the original, conceptual (but nonempirical) main categories,

tions. Client views and goals are comprehensively reported in the Profile and are taken into full consideration when the narrative data are coded. Nonetheless, the researcher may wish to obtain a family's own evaluation of the situation, which is at once a more direct and independent assessment than that of the interviewer. The attitudes of family members regarding their common life, values, and goals are significant because they constitute the material from which the helping sciences can gather an understanding of behavior and behavior change. In fact, knowledge about the client's views on treatment, a much neglected area of research, can be of key importance in service planning and execution. Indeed, it has been said again and again that service assessment is well nigh meaningless without obtaining the views of the client, who is, after all, the main object of any treatment endeavor.

There are, however, certain problems encountered when attempting to compare a family's evaluation of their own social functioning with that of the researcher's if the comparison is cross-sectional rather than longitudinal. First, there is the requirement that the family and the coder use the same coding scheme. It is unrealistic to expect any particular group of families to "buy" the evaluative frame of reference developed here, and it is equally undesirable to restrict the freedom of the family's independent evaluation by imposing a professional framework upon them.

These difficulties can be overcome, however, when change in functioning over time is studied, since change constitutes a modification of the situation, for better or worse, in terms of

---

such as family relationships and economic functioning, emerged from the principal-factor method of analysis intact, while others, such as Care and Training of Children, were split up among two factors: training and emotional care appeared as a variable on the expressive-interpersonal dimension, while physical care had its highest loading under instrumental functioning.

standards that are meaningful to the respondent as well as to
the researcher. Therefore, when examining the family's own
evaluation of social functioning the focus should be upon
change.

In order to obtain this kind of information from both client
and nonclient families, a schedule was constructed to measure
change in family functioning as perceived by the respondent.
Paralleling the Profile of Family Functioning, it contains
items organized by the same areas and subcategories. The total
number of items, all of which are structured, or closed, is forty-
nine, and their number per sub-category ranges from one to
five. This schedule is used to self-evaluate change occurring
over a particular time period that is clearly delineated in the
minds of the respondents. Time may be defined to the respondents, for example, as that period during which the family
received treatment services of one kind or another; it may be a
period that began with an event that was a landmark in family
history (wedding, birth of a first child, death of a family
member, drastic change in the family's economic fortunes,
etc.). Measurement of change, then, is retrospective, but its
potentially subjective character is mitigated by guidelines
along which change can be rated. Areas and subcategories—
paralleling the Profile of Family Functioning—in which
movement or change in functioning may have taken place, and
degrees of change—positive, negative, or zero—are specified in
the schedule. (See schedule Self-Evaluation of Family
Functioning in Appendix A.)

The schedule data can be statistically analyzed in a number
of ways, depending upon the score distribution. (The five-point
continuum bears no relationship to the seven levels of family
functioning discussed above; the present schedule deals only
with change in, and not the status of, social functioning.)
Change as registered by a family's self-evaluation can be
analyzed in terms of the five-point continuum given in the
schedule—if scores are well distributed—or in terms of a sim-

ple plus, zero, and minus pattern. If data are heavily skewed, further simplification in the form of score dichotomies is indicated, which can be accomplished by combining zero with positive or negative changes. Correlational analysis between the Family Profile and the self-evaluation data may then be carried out by areas and/or subcategories. At this point the self-evaluation schedule has been employed in two published studies (Geismar, Lagay, et al. 1972, pp. 159-166, 220-230; Geismar and Wolock). There is considerable convergence in the findings of our own studies and those of others (Beck and Jones 1973, pp. 90-108; Sacks, Bradley, and Beck, pp. 52-81) indicating a fair measure of agreement between client self-evaluation of change and the evaluation of others when global scores are used but low agreement on the details of that change.

Our own instrument for families' self-evaluation of change is given in Appendix A.

9.   Elaboration of the Family Functioning Scale to Meet Special Research Needs

In the development of the family-functioning scale every effort was made to construct data-collection categories that are comprehensive enough to encompass a wide variety of family structures and situations. Thus, the Outline for Profiling Family Functioning makes provisions for gathering information on one-parent families, non-family members living in the household, and quasimarital relationships with paramours. Beyond these variations there is often need for more detailed information in given areas or subareas because of the specific focus of a study.

For instance, research on families of retarded youths requires more detailed data than are provided in the outline on the children's developmental pattern and the parents' relationship to organizations and institutions concerned with the welfare of the retarded child. The same applies to situations where a family member has been institutionalized in a health or correctional facility for a prolonged period. For cases such as these there is need for including in the outline items that furnish information required by the specific research focus.

One of the more common research problems in family study relates to the behavior and development of minor children, either in the home or temporarily placed. Studies of this kind demand more extensive and more individualized information on each child than is called for by the category "Individual Behavior and Adjustment-Children." Because of the frequency of this research focus we have included in this volume an outline for rating the Individual Behavior and Adjustment of a child served by an agency (Appendix B). The data collection is organized under eleven headings of role performance. The Outline is followed by a Guideline for rating the child's social functioning on criteria that correspond to those used in evaluating the family as a whole.

10. A Simplified Method of Coding Family Functioning

The reader will have discovered that the measurement technique applied to the family-functioning data requires painstaking coding of the narrative data, preferably by two or more coders in order to ensure an acceptable level of reliability. If consistent levels of high reliability can be established for batches of three dozen or more cases, single-rater coding can take the place of multiple ratings provided that the researchers institute periodic quality-control checks to make sure that the level of reliability is being maintained over time.

Because of the high demands of this coding procedure on time and financial resources, we experimented with a simplified coding process that utilizes a structured form of 165 items (Appendix C) grouped by the conceptual categories of the Outline for Profiling Family Functioning. There are minimally two but a mean number of six items per subcategory of family functioning. The items are precoded in terms of whether a given type of behavior or situation occurs "almost always," "often," "sometimes," or "rarely or never." Values ranging from *1* to *4* are assigned depending on whether the relative frequency of occurrence denotes a desirable (high score) or undesirable (low score) situation. The values for areas and subcategories of family functioning are the arithmetic means for the respective units.

A person whose familiarity with a family situation extends over the areas covered by the Outline for Profiling Family Functioning is able to complete the precoded schedule in fifteen to twenty minutes. The values assigned to each item, subcategory, and area can then be transferred immediately to IBM cards and programmed for computer processing.

Because the precoded items comprise situations and types of functioning that are relatively typical of American family structure and function (see section 9 above), this shortened rating procedure may not lend itself to coding cases characterized by unusual deviance in composition or functioning. This is conjectural, however, since there has been no opportunity to test such cases for reliability.

Extensive tests have, on the other hand, been carried out in order to establish the correlation between the conventional method of coding and the precoded technique. Correlations for total scores between precoded schedules and the regularly coded forms ranged from (gamma) +.65 to +.72 (standard deviations ranged from .16 to .24) for four groups of families comprising a total of 117 cases (Geismar and Charlesworth). When main categories in the two forms were correlated for a sample of sixty young families, the Pearsonian *r* coefficient was +.77. The corresponding correlation for subcategories was likewise +.77. Clearly, there is every indication that the simplified method of coding yields comparable results at least when applied to groups of relatively normal families.

Analysis with the aid of the precoded short form yields values from *1* to *4*. This is in contrast to the *1* to *7* score range of the regularly coded schedule of family functioning. If comparability in terms of this manual's criteria of social adequacy from one population to another or between different programs of intervention is the goal, use of the postcoded technique is clearly indicated. Weighting the scores of the precoded forms according to the *1* to *7* scale range may represent an alternative to the more cumbersome method of coding, but such an approach requires empirical testing.

VI. Measuring Community
Functioning

1. Introduction

Before the turn of the century American social work was
already making attempts to establish communitywide practice. The Charity Organization Societies, confronted by a mul-
tiplicity of efforts all aimed at raising funds and providing
services, sought to bring order out of the confusion by establishing a measure of coordination among agencies. However,
community organization as a differentiated method of social-
work practice was not born until the 1920s. Early formulations
were broad in nature and centered on "reconstruction of the

small community . . . sustaining a democratic process, involving the citizen and the expert at the grass roots level, to make a viable creative entity out of the community" (M. Schwartz, p. 177). By the 1940s and '50s the chief emphasis in community organization had shifted to the coordination of welfare services to meet human need, particularly of the deprived population. Consequently, fund raising and work with community-welfare councils became significant foci in training community-organization practitioners.

More recently there has been a further shift, a movement toward an institutional approach in which social work in general and community organization in particular devote themselves to meeting the basic needs of the total population instead of confining themselves to the socially handicapped. Community organization in this context is concerned with social organization, power structure, and social change. This approach makes it possible for social work to utilize the community theory and research that come from the disciplines of sociology and social psychology.

In spite of social work's abiding concern with community needs and problems, there has been comparatively little research done on these subjects. Exceptions were the work of the social-survey movement that flourished during the first half of this century (Zimbalist, pp. 119–179) and the priority-of-needs studies much in vogue during the 1950s and early '60s (for a critique of the latter see Geismar and Lagay). The priority-of-needs approach was eventually abandoned under the impact of a nationwide movement that sought to give the consumer of services a greater share in determining their nature.

The social indicators approach (Freeman and Sheldon), which was given impetus by U.S. government interest and support (U.S. Department of Commerce, *Social Indicators* 1973, 1976), came into prominence in the mid-1960s and has considerable relevance for social planning and policy. Social indicators are quantitative measures—generally collected as time series—that reflect the scope and intensity of a social concern. The term social indicators has been closely linked to the quality-of-life movement. Social work has, up to this point, made only minimal use of social-indicators data, partly because they are generally collected for geographic units that do not coincide with social-work activities, and partly because the information yielded by social indicators covers only partly the data needs of the social-work field.

The community planner or organizer more often than not has to go beyond available community data, particularly in the study of community needs and problems. In order to obtain the needed program information it is frequently necessary to embark on a collection of new data by way of interviewing local residents, key informants, members of special-interest groups, and others able to furnish relevant input.

The study of community functioning as defined here is applied research because its objective is the collection and processing of data for the express purpose of dealing with issues and problems that arise out of the context of community life. As was suggested at the beginning of this manual, the study of community functioning is an attempt to utilize a common theoretical dimension in examining the needs and problems of different units of society. The community is a most significant subject of study for social work because it represents the larger social setting within which other objects of social-work intervention—individuals, families, social and recreational groups, institutions, etc.—come to life, develop, and function. Assessment of the behavior or functioning of these other units is incomplete without knowledge of the functioning of the larger system. The measurement focus of the instrument to be presented is need for professional intervention. A discussion of the theoretical background for the endeavor follows in the next section. Unlike the St. Paul Scale of Family Functioning, the Community Functioning Scale is a product that has been subjected only to limited methodological testing and application in substantive research. Both its methodology and use in actual studies will be discussed below.

2. *Theoretical Underpinings*

Before attempting to discuss the technique of measurement there is need to give further consideration to some of the theoretical premises underlying the evaluative approach. The development of theoretical frameworks that are useful for empirical study have been retarded by the vast number of definitions the term community has been given in the sociological literature. Because of this diversity in meaning a broad definition of community such as was evolved by Roland L. Warren is probably most useful, at least for research such as this with an applied or technology-oriented focus. Warren defined the community as "that combination of social units and systems which performs the major social function having locality relevance" (Warren 1963, p. 9). This definition conveniently avoids the problems of specifying size, geographic space, length and degree of contact, association of units and systems, and so forth. The community, according to Warren, represents an "organization of social activities to afford people daily local access to those broad areas of activity which are necessary in day-to-day living" (p. 9). He then proceeds to classify activities in terms of five major functions that are said to have locality relevance: (1) production-distribution-consumption; (2) socialization; (3) social control; (4) social participation; and (5) mutual support (pp. 9–10).

This manual follows Warren in making functions a central concept around which data are to be organized. At the same time it should be remembered that the function-focused approach is part of a broader theoretical stance, shown in Chapter III, which builds upon the social-systems concept. Functions, as stated earlier, are the processes that contribute to the continuity and ordered change of the system (see Chapter IV). The three basic systems goals of autonomy, integration, and viability have been shown to be applicable to the community as well as to the family and, presumably, to other social systems.

As a social system, the community differs from most others in the large number and different kinds of subsystems that it encompasses. This led Edward Moe to call it a system of systems (p. 29). Warren, however, makes clear that the main difference between community and other systems is not the existence of numerous and diverse subsystems but rather the way in which these relate to one another (Warren 1963, p. 49). In contrast to formal organizations, the subsystems in the community are not rationally or deliberately related to each other but simply coexist, for the most part, meeting a vast variety of needs. Some organizations and institutions, such as city councils and municipal committees and deparments are, of course, centrally connected. Many others, however, exist only in relation to the needs, interests, and goals of some of the community's citizens or groups and have no connection to the community system as a whole. Other subsystems, such as churches or banks, are part of a hierarchical and centrally organized structure whose center of operations is entirely outside the community.

Subsystems of the family, such as parents, siblings, or mother-daughter alliances, can be readily identified and their relationship to the family system can be easily assessed. Community subsystems are exceedingly variable with respect to structure, function, goals, and purposes, making it virtually impossible to study community functioning in a standardized way from the vantage point of the subsystems' tasks and functions. Therefore, the study of community functioning outlined here does not attempt to evaluate directly the actual subsystems or their functions but concerns itself instead with the way the performance of some basic tasks is viewed by the community. The community's perception of the performance of tasks is a reflection, as it were, of the way the community subsystems are functioning. The functions of the subsystems may be referred to—as was done in the family-functioning framework—as the functional prerequisites for the community system.

There is yet another reason for refraining from a direct assessment of subsystems in the study of community functioning. Their goals and functions, unlike those of parents or children, are not only infinitely variable but also poorly defined. It would be most difficult to reach any consensus on the "socially expected functions" of such diverse groups as chambers of commerce, P.T.A.'s, boards of education, antipoverty corporations, recreation councils, or churches. The present approach does not disregard the actual community subsystems; it merely avoids studying them directly and postulates instead the existence of certain universal community structures, such as the labor market, welfare organizations, educational services, or political parties, whose functioning can be evaluated indirectly through the attitudes of individuals in the community. These structures have their counterpart in the functional prerequisites of the system that enable the community to render the services needed by its population.

The postulation of community subsystems and the indirect measurement of their functioning serves a most important purpose in this study. Based upon the notion that there are certain universal functions that must be performed to meet the basic needs of any and all populations in every community, no matter how large or small, homogeneous or diversified, the present approach rates a community by whether or not, in one form or another, the functions have been carried out without investigating whether subsystems have actually been established to fulfill them.

Ideally, research on community functioning ought to be directly measuring the functioning of its component parts—as was done in relation to the family—through observation, questioning, examining records, and so forth. But in a structure as complex as a community, small as it might be, that would be a most formidable undertaking, calling for a very large investment in time and funds. Alternatively, the approach taken here of indirect measurement examines the extent to which services and resources deemed universally needed (at least in this society) meet the basic needs of community members. Like the study of the family, one of the underlying assumptions of community research is that the systems function to ensure their own continuity, and this relies in turn upon the achievement of their basic goals, defined earlier as autonomy, integration, and viability. Central to these are the needs of their constituents for material, biological, social, and emotional well-being. Therefore, a key indicant for assessing the quality of the community's social functioning is the extent to which services and resources satisfy the population. Community functioning, when operationalized, reads the judgment of community members as to the adequacy or inadequacy of the provisions for services, resources, and opportunities, which fall into two basic conceptual groupings: Primary Provisions for survival, maintenance of minimum level of social functioning, and basic socialization; and Secondary Provisions to achieve social participation, social control, mobility, social and political and cultural expression, and adequate instrumental living arrangements. Primary and Secondary Provisions are not sharply divided but differ mainly by degree of presumed urgency. The categorization rests upon the assumption that, in American society, income, employment, shelter, and social security meet more fundamental needs than social participation or social control, insofar as they refer to an individual's chance to live a satisfactory life. It must be borne in mind, nevertheless, that under certain conditions Secondary Provisions may become more salient than certain Primary ones. For instance, social control in the form of police protection may be more important than housing to a resident of the inner city with its high crime rate. Or the absence of public transportation (instrumental needs) may pose a more serious problem to low-income residents than poor schools (Primary Socialization), for if they cannot afford a private car and are unable to reach their job by means of public transportation, their family's livelihood is threatened. However, this writer argues that, by and large, Primary Provisions as identified in this study are more directly associated with the issue of survival than Secondary ones.

The relationship between the basic goals of social systems and Primary and Secondary Provisions to meet population needs in the community system is shown in Chart 3.

As the chart shows, provisions to meet the needs of population are, for the most part, integrative in nature, in the sense that they serve to unify and harmonize the constituent elements of the system while furthering its instrumental and expressive aims. Provisions for social control, however, such as protecting citizens against hazards and providing security to residents in times of crisis, enable the system to remain viable, while other forms of social control and provisions for derived instrumental needs, such as transportation and shopping facilities, enable the system to be autonomous.

In relating community functions or provisions for services, resources, and opportunities to the concept of need, we are focusing on some of the basic concerns of social-work practice. Need denotes a demand for gratification on one or more levels of behavior, biological, psychological, or social. If that gratification is not forthcoming, need may be said to prevail (it is sometimes also referred to as unmet need) and is generally considered to constitute a type of social problem (Geismar 1966, p. 231).

Need is a key concept, a term used by all methods of social work. Whether in casework, group work, or community organization, the practitioner is confronted with the task of identifying the needs of her or his clientele and then dealing with

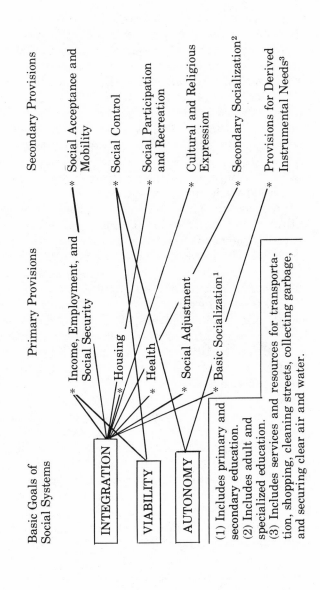

Chart 3   CONCEPTUAL FRAMEWORK FOR EVALUATING COMMUNITY FUNCTIONING

Functional Prerequisites of the Community System
(Organized by Areas of Provisions for Services, Resources,
and Opportunities to Meet Needs of Populations.)

Basic Goals of
Social Systems

Primary Provisions

Secondary Provisions

INTEGRATION

VIABILITY

AUTONOMY

* Income, Employment, and
  Social Security

* Housing

* Health

* Social Adjustment

* Basic Socialization[1]

* Social Acceptance and
  Mobility

* Social Control

* Social Participation
  and Recreation

* Cultural and Religious
  Expression

* Secondary Socialization[2]

* Provisions for Derived
  Instrumental Needs[3]

(1) Includes primary and
secondary education.
(2) Includes adult and
specialized education.
(3) Includes services and resources for transportation, shopping, cleaning streets, collecting garbage,
and securing clear air and water.

them according to their urgency, their priority for fulfillment, their potential for being satisfied by direct or indirect means, and the possible alternatives to their gratification. Needs are usually seen as the properties of an individual, family, or other small group. Societal values and norms, by contrast, provide the framework within which needs may be judged as being amenable to satisfaction (p. 231).

When relating need to the total community, the concept continues to apply to individuals and small groups, but we focus upon the extent to which it appears in the total system. Wide prevalence of need, need that is shared by most individuals or small groups within a given system and is, therefore, statistically definable, can be termed *need-consensus.*

It is possible for need and need-consensus to exist in an infinite number of behavior and functioning areas, so that categorizing needs would be a very ambitious undertaking. Therefore, for purposes of measurement we have identified a series of areas within which services, resources, and opportunities are made available to members of a community with an eye toward meeting a variety of biological, psychological, social, and material needs. The framework of categories is basically institutional, although it differentiates, as was pointed out earlier, between provisions (Primary) related to meeting survival needs and provisions (Secondary) aimed at satisfying needs assumed to be less crucial for human existence.

If need-consensus exists in a substantial number of areas of service provision, it is a sign of poor community functioning, signifying failure to meet the basic needs of a population. Need-consensus does not fix blame or responsibility for such failure, for it does not identify which structure or substructure was charged with meeting specific needs. There are, indeed, striking variations among communities with regard to the allocation of responsibility to external agencies, institutions, organizations, etc. The presence of need-consensus merely indicates that within a given community certain needs have not been met, and in this sense the community may be said to be malfunctioning. The question of identifying the particular subsystems that failed in their operations is a statutory one. On the American scene the responsibility for the welfare of community residents is shared by the municipality, the county, the state, and the federal government. The relative contributions of each differ widely, depending on a number of factors—size of community, local resources, the legislative framework of each type (federal to municipal) of authority. Only in the broadest sense can community malfunctioning be identified with community failure, namely, if we accept the assumption that political incorporation or self-government carries with it the moral and/or administrative responsibility to meet the needs of constituents.

A point made by this writer in an earlier paper must be stressed here, that "the goal of community functioning as formulated here is not an absolute state of performance, as implied in the concept of Utopia, but a situation where the actions and activities of the system meet the needs of its members (Geismar 1966, pp. 232-233).[9] Need-consensus reflects a gap, as it were, between the requirements for the welfare of residents and the actual ways in which they are met. Need and need-consensus are not absolutes but properties related to the psychosocial characteristics of the population. A crucial factor determining need is people's expectations, which in turn have been shaped by past experience, prevailing standards and norms, and available opportunities. The gap between requirements and resources is also relative in character because its magnitude is determined by the nature of a population's needs.

Two possible approaches could be used to measure the manner in which residents of communities have their needs met:

---

9.   I am indebted to Professor Albert Comanor of the University of Calgary for the idea expressed here.

(1) Determining the needs of community members and obtaining a personal assessment from each resident on the way in which his or her specific needs are being met by community services and resources; and (2) Gathering the views of community residents on the ways in which community members have their needs met, regardless of whether they themselves are actually experiencing any one need.

While it may seem that the first approach is the more precise and logical because it bases evaluation on direct personal experience, it requires an *a priori* determination of what each person's needs are—a most formidable undertaking. Age, sex, occupation, and place of residence provide some very sketchy guidelines indicating an individual's need for services and resources. They are rough indeed, for within each category of community membership need is also determined by intelligence, state of health, degree of social adjustment, and so forth. To make this first approach feasible it would be necessary to have the assessment of need-meeting be preceded by a comprehensive need study. Such an expensive and time-consuming undertaking would be justified if we had conclusive evidence that people are able to provide more valid data regarding the ways in which their own needs are being met than about the manner in which the needs of others are being satisfied. Lacking such evidence, the first approach, which would require the use of large samples in order to secure representatives from population groupings reflecting every kind of need, was abandoned. It was decided to adopt the second approach, which relies on an analysis of the responses of community members regarding every need for services and resources that had been identified in the study. To guard against meaningless answers, respondents have been encouraged to check the item "I know nothing about the subject" whenever they lack information about the way specific needs are being met.

To summarize, the present research studies community functioning by securing the responses of community residents—or a sample of residents—regarding the adequacy of basic provisions of services, resources, and opportunities to meet the needs of the population. We assume that meaningful responses can be obtained from most adults who have been living in a community and have been witness to the ways in which various needs are being met. Residents of a community may experience the functioning of services directly, as they or members of their families are served by educational, health, or welfare agencies, or indirectly, as relatives, friends, and neighbors share their experiences with them, or as they learn about others from the news media.

Validity in the evaluation of community functioning resides essentially in a correct assessment of the attitudes of residents about the way needs are being met. What is being evaluated is the reciprocal relationship between needs and resources, in other words, the system's ability to cope with such need as may be found in diverse areas of human functioning. Objection may be raised to the fact that such a definition of community functioning constitutes a highly subjective property. This subjectivity, however, does not of itself diminish validity as long as it is understood that we are not seeking to measure the actual organizational effectiveness or quality of services but the *beliefs* of the local population. It is not farfetched to assume that the beliefs are correlated with service quality when there is a need for services. However, such a correlation is not crucial to the success of the present evaluative endeavor and might appropriately become the subject of a separate study. Community functioning, as operationalized here, takes on its major significance as a variable that informs the researcher as to the population's views about the relationship between resources and needs. This variable represents a social fact that is of importance for those who plan and render, as well as for those who receive, services.

Chart 3, presented above, furnished the conceptual framework of the provisions for services, resources, and opportunities. It is organized into two area groupings, Primary and Secondary, according to the assumed urgency of needs, and into eleven areas of services, resources, and opportunities for meeting these population needs. Each area is composed of several items, ranging from two to ten in number, making a total of forty-two items. These items grouped by areas are given below:

A. PRIMARY PROVISIONS

1. *Income, Employment, and Social Security*

    Financial assistance for those who cannot work and have no other source of income, or do not earn enough

    Unemployment insurance

    Workers' compensation

    Social Security and pensions for the retired

    Jobs for all who are able to work

    Job finding, placement, and training

2. *Housing*

    Low-cost public housing

    Middle-income rental housing

    Less costly private housing

3. *Basic Socialization*

    Schools for children at the elementary and high-school level

    Special classes and services for children with learning problems

Job training for those who lack skills and education to hold a decent job

4. *Health*

Low-cost or free services of doctors and dentists, hospitals, clinics, and baby-keep-well stations

Private medical and dental services

Comprehensive medical insurance

5. *Social Adjustment*

Counseling and guidance services for people and families with problems

Treatment services and institutions for the mentally ill, alcoholics, drug addicts, and other seriously maladjusted persons

Facilities for children placed away from their homes, such as institutions, foster homes, etc.

Nursing homes for the elderly in need of constant care

Social and recreational services for the elderly

Rehabilitation services for the physically handicapped

Special educational and vocational services for the mentally retarded and brain damaged

Homemaker services for parents out of the home

Day-care centers and nurseries for the children of working parents

Parole, probation, and other services for delinquent youths and adults

B. SECONDARY PROVISIONS

6. *Social Acceptance and Mobility*

A chance for everyone to be fully accepted, regardless of race, color, or creed

Opportunities for all to get ahead economically and socially

7. *Social Control*

Protection against personal hazards and damage of all kinds through the services of the fire department, police department, courts, etc.

Legal protection regardless of ability to pay legal fees

Opportunities for political expression through voting, political organization, and other forms of democratic process

Opportunities to change things with which you are dissatisfied at the municipal level, by talking or writing to officials, staging protests, etc.

8. *Social Participation and Recreation*

Clubs, neighborhood centers, and other organizations offering social, recreational, and educational programs

Recreational facilities, such as parks, playgrounds, swimming pools, sports fields

9. *Secondary Socialization*

Provisions for higher and specialized education

Adult-education courses and programs

10. *Cultural and Religious Expression*

Opportunities for cultural and artistic pursuits

Opportunities for religious expression and participation

11. *Provisions for Derived Instrumental Needs*

Transportation Facilities (public or private) for getting to work, for shopping and social occasions

Shopping within easy reach

Efficient garbage collection and sewage facilities

Cleaning and maintenance of roads and sidewalks

Clean air and water and an otherwise pollution-free environment.

This selection of items was accomplished by two preliminary studies: the first sought to identify issues of concern to the community welfare planner (Nover, Pollak, et al.), and the second compared the attitudes of those who plan services with those who consume them (Geismar and Lagay, pp. 76-93). In the course of these studies it became clear that elite groups and rank-and-file members of the community do not necessarily agree upon social-welfare needs. The two studies led to the creation of a list of items that appeared relevant for respondents living in a medium-sized urban community. Further testing and modification of the items was brought about by two community needs-and-action studies with random samples of young urban families in two metropolitan communities (Geismar 1973, pp. 163-175; and Geismar and Geismar, Chapter 8). The final scale product presented here is, of course, not truly final. It is the array of provisions identified as meeting common human needs in an urban seaboard area. Other parts of the United States may reflect the same type of need structure and may, therefore, be researched effectively with the aid of the present instrument, or they may have different need structures making instrument modifications necessary.

In concluding this section there is need to emphasize that the study of community functioning by way of assessing provisions for services, resources, and opportunities to meet need is research into the system's performance, measured against a hypothetical model of service structure that meets universal (within this cultural setting) human needs. What the research sets out to determine is the nature of the reciprocal relationship between requirements for services and the community's provisions to satisfy them. The methodology for studying this relationship utilizes the views of consumers or potential consumers of services, for they reflect unambiguously the success or failure of the community welfare enterprise.

3. Rating Procedure and Collection of Data Covering Related Variables

The study of community functioning, in contrast to that of family functioning (except for the new procedure introduced in this revised edition), uses a precoded instrument that obviates the need for coders and rating criteria. Responses to the community-functioning questionnaire are given on a four-point Likert-type continuum. Respondents are asked to check whether, in relation to various kinds of needs, they consider services, resources, and opportunities as being

(1)   Adequate as they are or not needed;
(2)   Less than adequate, some improvement needed;
(3)   Less than adequate, great improvement needed;
(4)   Entirely lacking or wholly inadequate, urgently needed.

Forty-two questionnaire items are grouped by the conceptual categories presented above without any headings being shown in the instrument itself. The grouping was not seen as promoting a respondent acquiescence, since conceptually related items in each area are yet quite distinct from one another and require the interviewee to respond to discrete, specific stimuli. The response category (5), "I know nothing about the subject," is designed to reduce the likelihood of gathering opinions on a need-service dimension with which the respondent is unfamiliar.

The schedule presented here allows for the gathering of some data beyond the forty-two items (numbers 7-48) covering the provision of services, resources, and opportunities dimension. These data, the collection of which is optional for the researcher concerned exclusively with exploring social-welfare (in the broadest sense) aspects of community functioning, cover a number of demographic and attitudinal variables that are theoretically relevant to the study of community provisions to meet population needs.

Demographic variables covering age, sex, marital status, number of children, education, occupation, religion, race, and length of residence in the community are dealt with by schedule items 60-70. Item number 80 permits the coding, according to any number of systems to be selected by the researcher, of type of socioeconomic status of respondent. Schedule items 1-6 are set aside for identifying the respondent, her/his neighborhood (optional), and the particular community in which the study was done.

Social and political participation and use of community health and welfare services are dealt with by items 71-79. Information about these subjects would appear to be relevant when exploring the connection between attitude toward the existing service structure and involvement in and/or with community organizations and agencies. It can be argued that such involvement is likely to affect a person's perception of a community's functioning and modify his or her attitudes toward the adequacy of services and resources. Of course, one's perception can be affected in two ways: the volunteer worker, especially one who is a member of an elite group, may see the performance of community services in a more favorable light than does the uninvolved person. Use of agencies rendering high-quality services may have the same effect. By contrast, experience with an agency that provides poor services is likely to color negatively the views of a respondent toward the local service structure.

Another dimension covered in the questionnaire, "measures that are likely to get results to the extent that changes in the service structure are considered desirable" (items 49-59), can be viewed as both an independent and dependent variable in the study of community functioning. This dimension is made up of items denoting different means to attain desired goals, ranging from the conventional and generally accepted—such as voting and writing letters to legislators—to the innovative and deviant: organizing new groups and holding demonstrations, both violent and nonviolent.

It is hypothesized that people's beliefs regarding their chances of bringing about desired changes in the service structure tend to color their views about the quality of services. Belief in the efficacy of conventional and nondeviant methods is thought to foster more favorable opinions about the adequacy of services relative to need. Correlatively, a negative attitude toward the service structure is likely to give rise to the advocacy of innovative and deviant means of effecting change. Whatever the actual nature of the postulated causal relationship, the demonstration of an existing association between the two variables can be of considerable significance for service planning, which, if it is to be effective, must address itself to the social and political aspirations of the population.

Whereas coding of the community-functioning data is already built into the structure of the scale and requires no further rating efforts, the analysis of the data present a series of options determined, at least in part, by the service-need response patterns of the population tested. Heterogeneous response distributions, which approximate the normal curve on most items, make analysis by each response item on the five-point continuum possible, especially when the study comprises sizable samples. More homogeneous distributions require decisions to group responses trichotomously or dichotomously, the latter being a statistical accommodation to minimum data variability. Although the conceptual scheme presented above has provided a useful framework for collecting items and ordering them preliminarily in the analysis, the use of large, representative study samples should afford an opportunity to carry out scale refinement and simplification by factor analysis and related methods.

The questionnaire for collecting data on community functioning is given below. The schedule has been precoded for immediate IBM card punching and computer processing. Appropriate coding systems will have to be selected for items 66, 67, and 80.

COMMUNITY STUDY QUESTIONNAIRE

The Rutgers University Graduate School of Social Work is doing a study on community needs and community action. The purpose of this study is to get a better idea about the needs and wishes of the population with regard to the social services of the community. A further goal of the study is to convey to community leaders and planners the views of citizens on the subject of social services, in the hope that the findings of the study will contribute toward better planning and programming.

To make this study possible we are requesting about half an hour of your time to answer some questions on need for services and ways of bringing about desired changes in the services. The basic question we are asking you is this:

HOW SATISFACTORY ARE EACH ONE OF THE COMMUNITY SERVICES, RESOURCES, AND OPPORTUNITIES LISTED BELOW?

The services, resources, and opportunities listed here are generally considered important to the health and welfare of the community. Some are provided by the community itself, others are furnished by the county, the state, the federal government, or local and national voluntary organizations. Regardless of who provides the services, we should like you to express your thoughts and feelings about each type of service, resource, and opportunity. Which of the five answers below best represents your own opinion on each subject?

Services, resources, and opportunities are:

(1)   Adequate as they are or are not needed:

(2)   Less than adequate, some improvement needed:

(3)   Less than adequate, great improvement needed;

(4)   Entirely lacking or wholly inadequate, urgently needed;

(5)   I really do not know anything about that particular subject.

In selecting one answer or another you should be guided by what you believe the situation is in your community regardless of whether or not you and your family needs or has ever used such a service. Your reply will of course be influenced by any experience you may have had with the service, but beyond that your opinion is most likely to be determined by the experiences of relatives, friends, acquaintances, and neighbors, and by what you hear on the radio, see on T.V., or read in the newspaper or in magazines. Regardless of the source of information it is *your* point of view we are interested in.

In reading the items you may say that you do not have all the pertinent information. That may be correct, but none of us has *all* the pertinent information. We simply form an opinion on the basis of what we have learned. To know *your* opinion is very important to us. At the same time, we wish to assure you that all information you give us will be treated with complete confidentiality.

Finally, one last point. Before selecting one of the answers consider first whether there is need in the community for a given service. If there is need for a given service your answer is determined by how well the services, resources, or opportunities meet that need. If there is no need for a service, the proper answer is the first one, "services are adequate as they are or are not needed."

In the hope that we have succeeded in conveying to you the goals of our study we are asking you to check one but only one of the answers to each item listed below. Select answer number (5) only when you know nothing about the service mentioned. Repeating the question again, we should like you to tell us:

HOW SATISFACTORY ARE EACH ONE OF THE SERVICES, RESOURCES, AND OPPORTUNITIES IN YOUR COMMUNITY?

Please check items in the appropriate column, beginning with question 7 on the next page.

DO NOT FILL IN

(For research coder only)

1. _____ Community

2. _____ I.D. Number

3. _____

4. _____

5. _____

6. _____

SERVICES, RESOURCES, AND OPPORTUNITIES

	(1) Adequate as they are or not needed	(2) Some improvement needed	(3) Great improvement needed	(4) Entirely lacking or wholly inadequate; urgently needed	(5) I know nothing about the subject
7. Financial assistance for those who can't work and have no other source of income or don't earn enough					
8. Unemployment insurance					
9. Workers' compensation					
10. Social Security and pensions for the retired					
11. Jobs for all who are able to work					
12. Job finding, placement, and training					
13. Low-cost public housing					

14. Middle-income rental housing

15. Less costly private housing

16. Schools for children at the elementary and high-school level

17. Special classes and services for children with learning problems

18. Job training for those who lack skills and education to hold a decent job

19. Low-cost or free services of doctors and dentists, hospitals, clinics, and baby-keep-well stations

20. Private medical and dental services

21. Comprehensive medical insurance

22. Counseling and guidance services for people and families with problems

SERVICES, RESOURCES, AND OPPORTUNITIES

	(1) Adequate as they are or not needed	(2) Some improvement needed	(3) Great improvement needed	(4) Entirely lacking or wholly inadequate; urgently needed	(5) I know nothing about the subject
23. Treatment services and institutions for the mentally ill, alcoholic, drug addict, and other seriously maladjusted persons					
24. Facilities for children placed away from their homes, such as institutions, foster homes, etc.					
25. Nursing homes for the elderly in need of constant care					
26. Social and recreational services for the elderly					
27. Rehabilitation services for the physically handicapped					

28. Special educational and vocational services for the mentally retarded and brain damaged

29. Homemaker services for parents out of the home

30. Day-care centers and nurseries for the children of working parents

31. Parole, probation, and other services for delinquent youths as well as adults

32. A chance for everyone to be fully accepted regardless of race, color, or creed

33. Opportunities for all to get ahead economically and socially

34. Protection against personal hazards and damage of all kinds through the services of the fire department, police department, courts, etc.

35. Legal protection regardless of ability to pay legal fees

SERVICES, RESOURCES, AND OPPORTUNITIES

	(1) Adequate as they are or not needed	(2) Some improvement needed	(3) Great improvement needed	(4) Entirely lacking or wholly inadequate; urgently needed	(5) I know nothing about the subject
36. Opportunities for political expression, through voting, political organization, and other forms of democratic process					
37. Opportunities to change things with which you are dissatisfied at the municipal level by talking or writing to officials, staging protests, etc.					
38. Clubs, neighborhood centers, and other organizations offering social, recreational, and educational programs					
39. Recreational facilities, such as parks, playgrounds, swimming pools, sports fields, etc.					

40. Provisions for higher and specialized education

41. Adult-education courses and programs

42. Opportunities for cultural and artistic pursuits

43. Opportunities for religious expression and participation

44. Transportation facilities (public or private) for getting to work, for shopping and social occasions

45. Shopping within easy reach

46. Efficient garbage-collection sewage facilities

47. Cleaning and maintenance of roads and sidewalks

48. Clean air and water and an otherwise pollution-free environment

To the extent that you believe changes in services, resources, and opportunities in your community are needed, which of the measures listed below is most likely to get results?

	(1) Generally gets results	(2) Sometimes gets results	(3) Seldom gets results	(4) I don't know
49. *Letters* to legislators, city and government officials				
50. *Phone calls* to legislators, city and government officials				
51. *Personal visits* to City Hall, legislators, other officials				
52. Obtaining *Legal Help*				
53. *Organizing* neighborhood groups or groups of interested people				
54. Action through *existing groups*, like church groups, clubs, unions, political parties, action groups				
55. Newspaper *publicity* and other forms of publicity				

	(1) Generally gets results	(2) Sometimes gets results	(3) Seldom gets results	(4) I don't know
56. *Nonviolent* demonstrations				
57. *Violent* demonstrations				
58. Using *influential people* with pull				
59. *Voting*				

In conclusion, we would appreciate a little information about yourself, not to identify you as a person, but rather to enable us to relate the views you expressed to your social characteristics.

60. Your age

(1) ——— Under 18 (4) ——— 36–45 (7) ——— 66–75
(2) ——— 18–25 (5) ——— 46–55 (8) ——— 76 and over
(3) ——— 26–35 (6) ——— 56–65 (BL) ——— N.K. (Not Known)

61. Sex

(1) ——— Male
(2) ——— Female

62. Marital Status

(1) ——— Single (3) ——— Widowed (5) ——— Separated
(2) ——— Married (4) ——— Divorced (BL) ——— N.K.

63. Number of children (1) _____ None
                          (2) _____ One
                          (3) _____ Two
                          (4) _____ Three
                          (5) _____ Four
                          (6) _____ Five
                          (7) _____ Six
                          (8) _____ Seven
                          (9) _____ Eight or more
                          (0) _____ Not applicable
                          (BL) _____ N.K.

Number of years of school completed

64. *Yourself*   65. *Your spouse*

(1) _____   Under 7 years of school   (1) _____
(2) _____   7–9 years of school   (2) _____
(3) _____   10–11 years of school   (3) _____
(4) _____   High-school graduate   (4) _____
(5) _____   1–3 years of college (also business   (5) _____
                 school)
(6) _____   Four-year college graduate   (6) _____
(7) _____   Professional (M.A., M.S., M.E., M.D.,   (7) _____
                 Ph.D., Ed.D., M.S.W., L.L.B., D.D., etc.)
(0) _____   Special schools attended beyond   (0) _____
                 eighth grade
(BL) _____   Not Applicable or not known   (BL) _____

Occupation (give job title, type of organization you work for and describe briefly what you are doing. If retired or unemployed list the last job).

66. *Your own*   67. *Your spouse*

_____   _____
_____   _____

DO NOT FILL IN

Codes for items. (For research coder only.)

66. (1) _____	67. (1) _____
(2) _____	(2) _____
(3) _____	(3) _____
(4) _____	(4) _____
(5) _____	(5) _____
(6) _____	(6) _____
(7) _____	(7) _____
(8) _____	(8) _____
(9) _____	(9) _____
(0) _____ Not Applicable	(0) _____ Not Applicable
(BL _____ N.K.	(BL) _____ N.K.

68. Religion   (1) _____ Catholic   (4) _____ Other
                (2) _____ Protestant   (5) _____ None
                (3) _____ Jewish   (BL) _____ N.K.

69. Race   (1) _____ Black   (5) _____ Other
                (2) _____ White   (BL) _____ N.K.
                (3) _____ Puerto Rican
                (4) _____ Chicano

70. Length of time you have lived in the community
    (1) _____ Less than a year
    (2) _____ One year to two years
    (3) _____ More than two years to three years
    (4) _____ More than three years to four years
    (5) _____ More than four years to five years
    (6) _____ More than five years to ten years
    (7) _____ More than ten years to fifteen years
    (8) _____ More than fifteen years to twenty years
    (9) _____ More than twenty years to thirty years
    (0) _____ More than thirty years
    (BL) _____ N.K.

Number of clubs or organizations, if any, to which you and your spouse belong (do not include political party, church, synagogue or union membership but do list church clubs, union clubs, and professional associations).

71. *Yourself*		72. *Your spouse*
(1) _____	None	(1) _____
(2) _____	One	(2) _____
(3) _____	Two	(3) _____
(4) _____	Three	(4) _____
(5) _____	Four	(5) _____
(6) _____	Five	(6) _____
(7) _____	Six or more	(7) _____
(0) _____	Not Applicable	(0) _____
(BL) _____	N.K.	(BL) _____

Do you or your spouse hold office in one or more clubs or organizations (not including political party, union, or church)?

73. *Yourself*		74. *Your Spouse*
(1) _____	Not an officer	(1) _____
(2) _____	In one club or organization	(2) _____
(3) _____	In two	(3) _____
(4) _____	In three	(4) _____
(5) _____	In four	(5) _____
(6) _____	In five	(6) _____
(7) _____	In six or more	(7) _____
(0) _____	Not Applicable (belongs to no club)	(0) _____
(BL) _____	N.K.	(BL) _____

Are your or your spouse registered members of a political party?

75. *Yourself*		76. *Your spouse*
(1) _____	Not a member	(1) _____
(2) _____	Member of Democratic Party	(2) _____
(3) _____	Member of Republican Party	(3) _____
(4) _____	Member of another party	(4) _____
(0) _____	Not Applicable	(0) _____
(BL) _____	N.K.	(BL) _____

Do you and your spouse generally vote in political elections—local, state, or national?

77. *Yourself*		78. *Your spouse*
(1) _____	Never vote	(1) _____
(2) _____	Rarely vote	(2) _____
(3) _____	Occasionally vote	(3) _____
(4) _____	Generally vote	(4) _____
(5) _____	Always vote	(5) _____
(0) _____	Not Applicable	(0) _____
(BL) _____	N.K.	(BL) _____

79. Have you or members of your family ever used any of the local community health and welfare services or facilities listed below?

(1) _____ Used none of them
(2) _____ Used one of them infrequently
(3) _____ Used one of them a number of times
(4) _____ Used two of them, both infrequently
(5) _____ Used two of them, at least one a number of times
(6) _____ Used three or more of them
(BL) _____ N.K.

Please check as many of the services as you have used

_____ Counseling and mental health
_____ Group work, social and recreational
_____ Clinics and hospital outpatient
_____ Public assistance
_____ Vocational training and rehabilitation
_____ Public housing
_____ Homemaker
_____ Day care for children
_____ Placement and foster homes
_____ Nursing homes for the elderly
_____ Social-rehabilitation services for people with special problems and needs
_____ Correctional (parole, probation, etc.)
_____ Others, please indicate _____

We are most grateful to you for giving us time to pose the many questions and note your opinions on subjects under study. We wish to assure you again that the information you provided will be treated confidentially.

DO NOT FILL IN (FOR RESEARCH CODER ONLY)

80. Index of Social Position of Family

(1) _____
(2) _____
(3) _____
(4) _____
(5) _____
(6) _____
(7) _____
(8) _____
(9) _____
(0) _____ Not Applicable
(BL) _____ N.K.

4. Reliability and Validity

Although the Community Functioning Scale has gone through a number of time-consuming stages of development, it has only been given a limited field test, and data on reliability and validity are still in short supply. A reliability test-retest was carriedout with a group of fifty respondents, and an inter-community comparison of scale scores, obtained from random samples of interviewees, was examined for first evidence on scale validity.

The test-retest method is one of the most conclusive means of establishing the reliability or consistency over time of opinions held by respondents. Its value as a reliability index is limited by the problem of finding subjects willing to take the test twice. The idea of repeated administration of the same instrument is generally abandoned precisely because "guinea pigs" willing to promote social methodology—in contradistinction to people who are ready to contribute their views as a means of building knowledge—are not thought to abound. The problem can undoubtedly be overcome by motivating potential respondents with better incentives than "a chance to advance methodology," namely, material rewards. But the additional expense involved is usually sufficient reason for the investigator to seek other ways to test reliability.

This investigator chose the path of well-known compromise, using college students, who, one hopes, are motivated to contribute their services because they can be persuaded by the "appeal to science" approach and, alternatively, are likely to cooperate because of the pressures they feel are being exerted by their instructors. Two classes of students in the Rutgers Graduate School of Social Work were used as subjects. The classes were of unequal size, numbering thirty-six and twenty-four, respectively. The first class was made up of entering students who had had a limited amount of class work and no field experience. The second group was composed of students who had completed one year of work and whose method of specialization was community organization.

The first group was thought to be more nearly like the typical respondent asked to take the community-functioning schedule, for they had had no training in identifying and assessing community problems, skills that might conceivably be correlated with the stability of attitudes on the subject. This group of students differed, however, from the rank and file of potential respondents in level of education (they were graduate students) and interest in the subject of community needs and problems. The second group had completed three-fourths of their coursework and two-thirds of their fieldwork as professionals in training at a community organization agency. The first group was asked to complete the schedules by describing the situation prevailing in their home communities. The second group faced the task of rating the communities in which they were completing their second semester of fieldwork.

While response patterns of neither group could be viewed as being representative of a community population, they were thought to reveal, when compared with each other, the extent to which knowledge of the subject would tend to influence the stability of attitudes. Differences between beginning and advanced students, it was believed, would permit inferences about possible differences between the student population tested here and community residents included in studies but not in the reliability test.

The approach to the test-retest experiment was as follows: the students were asked to participate in a little study, aimed at comparing the prevalence of need for services in various New Jersey communities. A week later they were approached again with the request to complete the schedule a second time, and the purpose of the repeated administration of the questionnaire was revealed to them.

It was assumed that the passing of a week reduces the likelihood that the respondent will recall exactly how he or she answered the questions on the first test. Further postponement in taking the retest, it is believed, may invalidate the test-retest idea because changes in the community situation may bring about a change in opinions registered. As it turned out, the first group was administered the second test ten days later because of a change in class schedule. Most members of Group 2 took the second test a week after the first, but four took it two to three weeks later because of absences.

In view of the fact that one student or another could not be reached both times, the sample size was reduced to thirty-one in Group 1 and nineteen in Group 2, leaving a total of fifty sets of usable questionnaires. Each set is being compared in rela-

tion to changes from one administration to the next in terms of
the following alternatives of change on the five point scale:

(1)   Respondent checked the same answer both times.

(2)   Respondent checked a different answer one scale step
      removed.

(3)   Respondent checked a different answer two or more
      scale steps removed. This includes a check of one of the
      four alternatives of service needs (1-4) and the other a
      check of "I know nothing about the subject" (5).

The answer to the question of differences in reliability rates
due to respondent's knowledge of subject was given by almost
identical rates (63.5% and 63.3%) for Groups 1 and 2 on "identical response" patterns. This finding made it possible to combine samples from the first and second test for the further
analysis of the consistency of responses.

The mean item reliability (covering forty-one schedule
items[10]) was 63.41% with a standard deviation of 6.87. That is
to say, the average percentage for "no change" responses was
63, but the range was 80% to 50% from the most to the least
reliable item, with about two-thirds of the items showing a
range between 57% and 70%. The mean percentage for one-
point changes (either upward or downward) was 30.68. This
left a residual mean percentage of 5.91 for items registering
shifts of more than one scale point or shifts from a substantive
response to a "don't know" answer, or the reverse.

When the test-retest analysis is extended to individuals

10.   The forty-second item, "Clean air and water and an otherwise
pollution-free environment," was added after completion of the reliability study in the wake of more recent community-needs surveys that
revealed the subject of pollution as a high-priority issue for action.

rather than items, we obtain a mean of 63.3% with a standard deviation of 18.9%. This indicates that the average (mean) respondent was consistent from one administration of the test to another on nearly two-thirds of the items. The range of response patterns extended from 100% (respondent was consistent on every item) to 27% (respondent was consistent on only about a fourth of the items). Two-thirds of the respondents, as shown by the standard deviation, were consistent on 82% to 44% of the items. For those respondents who changed their scale position one or more points from the first to the second test, the up-and-down movement was reasonably well balanced. The mean upward movement was 15.2% and the mean downward shift 16.2%; in other words, slightly more of the items were scored lower than were scored higher the second time the questionnaire was filled out.

This test-retest reliability is only marginally satisfactory. The reliability ratio, however, can be improved considerably by simplifying the data analysis in a manner that reduces the substantive four-point scale (responses 1-4) to a dichotomy. This can be done after analyzing the nature of the distribution and determining the optimal cut-off point. Dichotomizing responses in terms of high or low, or those advocating change versus those not advocating it—whichever is statistically most useful—is likely to boost reliability substantially. The present reliability study did not permit this type of analysis because the schedule was completed by respondents who were addressing themselves to different communities, and this did not allow for an overall meaningful grouping of responses.

Instrument validity is an infinitely more complex issue than reliability. In the case of the Community Functioning Scale it denotes a correspondence between scale scores and the actual beliefs of community members regarding the adequacy of services and resources to meet needs in their community. The tapping of these beliefs was the express purpose for constructing the Community Functioning Scale. The most direct way of determining the validity of scale results would be to compare with the results of another, independent measure of community attitudes. This writer, however, is not aware of the existence of such a measure and undoubtedly would have refrained from developing the present tool had another, roughly comparable one been available.

The validity question could be approached by taking a second tack. It could be assumed that people's beliefs are highly correlated with actual conditions and that, therefore, known differences in conditions ought to correspond to measured scale differences. This assumption would seem to be reasonably defensible providing the populations that are being measured are roughly comparable. The reservation put forth in the last sentence rests on the contention that different populations, one native-born and the other new immigrants, or one lower class and the other middle class, would not necessarily react in a similar fashion to given social structures.

The first validity test of the Community Functioning Scale undertook to compare random samples of respondents from two New Jersey communities, New Brunswick and Newark, where populations are approximately 40,000 and 400,000, respectively. Despite size differences, both cities are characterized by a high rate of unemployment,[11] substandard housing,[12] low median family income,[13] and a high ratio of nonwhite minority

---

11.   The Newark estimate at the time of the study (1967) was 19.1% (Chernick, Indik, and Sternlieb, p. 11). The 1960 census listed the New Brunswick rate as 5.6%.

12.   Fourteen percent of New Brunswick homes were rated as substandard in 1960 (Georgina Smith [4] p. 16). A third of Newark houses were judged to be dilapidated (Brooks, p. 8).

13.   Seventeen percent of Newark's households reported family incomes of less than $3,000 a year in 1966 (Chernick, et al., p. 13). The 1959 rate for New Brunswick was 15.3 (Georgina Smith [a], p. 16).

220   Family and Community Functioning

groups[14] and foreign-born residents.[15] On these and other socioeconomic indexes both cities present a picture of social deprivation and urban decay, and both have experienced racial riots. The problem is more severe in Newark, as most of the indexes show; the difference, while due to many factors, is at least partly a function of size. The much greater magnitude of the difficulties—racial ghettoes, blighted housing, people who are unable to find jobs, abandoned cars in the streets, etc.— gives the city of Newark an air of despair, which is less pronounced in New Brunswick. Because of geographic location and population size, the latter city retains some suburban features that, in the minds of American urbanites, tend to be associated with the good life.

In the light of the situation described above, two hypotheses are formulated for testing the validity of the Community Functioning Scale:

(1)   The state of social deprivation in both communities is reflected in the views of the population and results in an overwhelming expression of attitudes strongly favoring changes in provisions for services, resources, and opportunities.

(2)   The perceived differentials in social and economic characteristics between Newark and New Brunswick will result in a stronger endorsement by Newark residents of the need for changes in service provisions.

---

14.   Negroes were reported to comprise 52% of the population of Newark in 1967. Nearly 10% were Spanish speaking, mainly Puerto Rican (Chernick, et al., p. xi). The percentage of Negroes and Puerto Ricans in New Brunswick was 37.0 and 12.1, respectively, in 1960 and presumed to be much higher near the end of the 1960s, when the study was done (Georgina Smith 1967 [a], pp. 17–18).

15.   The 1960 rates for foreign-born were 12% for Newark (Georgina Smith [b], p. 12) and 14% for New Brunswick (Georgina Smith [a], p. 18).

Newark data on community functioning were gathered from a sample of 315 housewives who were part of a larger study on the longitudinal social functioning of young families (Geismar 1973). This sample represented an 89% response of the 352 families originally selected as a probability sample,[16] those who remained with the research project to the end. The New Brunswick data comprised sixty-nine heads of households, two-thirds of them women, drawn randomly as a 1% random sample of households listed in the city directory. The attrition rate, due to refusals and the inability of interviewers to find people at home, was about 40%.

The mean rate at which respondents favored changes in the provisions for services (response alternatives 2, 3, or 4),[17] was 83.5% in Newark and 75.2% in New Brunswick. The respective mean percentages for Primary Provisions were 86.8 and 80.23. For Secondary Provisions they were 77.9% and 64.6%, respectively. A comparison of areas for the two cities revealed the distribution shown in Table 1.

The results of the comparison give unequivocal support to the two hypotheses. In both communities more than three-fourths of the respondents favored changes in service provisions. Newark citizens were stronger advocates of change in all areas, although in one—housing—the difference was too minuscule to be cited in support of the hypothesis. Striking differences between the two communities are apparent in pro-

---

16. The original sample was drawn from the universe of all young mothers under 30 who gave birth to a first child in 1964 and the first third of 1965. For details see Geismar, Lagay, et al., pp. 16-34).

17. The response alternative excluded from this tally is: *services, resources, and opportunities are adequate as they are.*

18. The reasons for the lack of difference in housing are not entirely clear. They might be explained by a higher level of aspiration in New Brunswick, set by the superior quality of housing in surrounding communities.

Table 1 PERCENTAGE OF RESPONDENTS ENDORSING CHANGE IN SERVICES AND RESOURCES IN NEWARK AND NEW BRUNSWICK

	Newark	New Brunswick
	Percent endorsing change	Percent endorsing change
PRIMARY PROVISIONS		
Income, Employment, and Social Security	85.4*	75.1
Housing	88.4	87.9
Basic Socialization	91.3	71.0
Health	81.8	75.0
Social Adjustment	90.0	86.1
SECONDARY PROVISIONS**		
Social Control	84.1	80.1
Social Participation and Recreation	91.7	68.6
Secondary Socialization	72.3	59.7
Provisions for Derived Instrumental Needs	68.9	53.1

*Differences between these Newark figures and those shown in the 1971 edition, mostly of the magnitude of one percentage point or less, are due to a different system of weighting items.

**The two areas of Social Acceptance and Mobility and Cultural and Religious Expression are excluded from this comparison because they were not contained in the schedule administered in Newark.

visions for social participation and recreation and basic socialization, which reflect the absence or inaccessibility of parks and playgrounds as well as substandard public schools in the city of Newark.

There are enough shortcomings in size and selection procedures of the two samples to recommend caution in the acceptance of the findings on validity. This writer would argue, nonetheless, that this first test, while not conclusive, constitutes overcoming the first major hurdle on that most difficult and studiously avoided validity tract. Further experimentation in reliability and validity testing is the principal mandate to the future user of the Community Functioning Scale.

5. Use of the Community Functioning Scale

The assessment of community functioning emerges as a rather anemic effort when compared to the measuring of family functioning—a seemingly strange situation, since it is obvious that the community is so much more complex a system. From a common-sense point of view, it would seem that the respective measurement endeavors would reflect the complexities of the areas for which they were designed, and yet precisely the opposite turns out to be the case. A rather involved technique was devised for measuring the small and relatively simple social system called *family,* while an uncomplicated method of measurement was prepared for the extremely complex structure known as *community.* The answer to this paradox lies in the following observation: a simple system allows itself to be studied in depth, whereas a complicated one defies all but gargantuan efforts at comprehensive and thorough evaluation. Does this statement imply then that the more unsophisticated effort reported here is actually of questionable utility? This writer believes that the measurement of community functioning by assessing attitudes toward services, resources, and opportunities serves a distinct purpose, for it contributes significantly to the fields of community planning and organization. It may, on the other hand, be of lesser importance to the many other disciplines associated with community study and practice.

It is well to remember that the complexity of the community system stems from the fact that it encompasses a vast number of subsystems, themselves differing enormously in size, tenure, and structure. Many of these, such as the business and industrial system, the health system, the housing system, and the educational system, fall within the purview of distinct and separate disciplines that require special expertise for their study. Any measurement endeavor that seeks to investigate the effectiveness of these subsystems would necessarily take a multidiscipline form. The greatest problem and also the special challenge in such an undertaking would be to tie specialized inquiries together into an integrated whole. At the present underdeveloped state of cross-discipline research in the social and behavioral sciences, the notion of intensively studying community functioning is doubtless premature and clearly beyond the mandate this writer has set for himself.

A more modest and, at this point, less utopian approach to researching community functioning is suggested by the study of social indicators. These indicators are measures designed to reflect the nature and changing character of social situations and processes. In the words of Raymond A. Bauer, social indicators "enable us to assess where we stand and are going with respect to our values and goals and to evaluate specific programs and determine their impact," (Bauer [a], p. 1). An impressive volume by Eleanor B. Sheldon and Wilbert E. Moore deals with social indicators and the study of social change. While the authors are mainly concerned with monitoring change by analyzing trends in populations, stratification, the family, the economy, religion, politics, and a host of other institutions, they make clear that their purpose is not program evaluation, but that it is "heavily weighted toward the scholarly, or analytic, side of the balance between theoretical and practical concerns focusing on large scale structural change" (Sheldon and Moore, p. 4). Bauer, by contrast, stresses the use of indicators to improve the state of the nation and achieve national goals. The social-indicators technique as a measure of system performance, well-being, and public percep- tions (U.S. Department of Commerce 1976, p. xxiv) is featured in two major publications of the U.S. Department of Commerce (1973, 1976) and in the research of Andrews and Withey (1976). The work of the Urban Institute in Washington, D.C., is a good example of the use of social indicators as a measure of quality of life at a community level (Flax).

Whichever purpose suits the researcher, it is obvious that the social-indicators movement has great potential for com- munity analysis. It holds promise for developing criteria to judge performance in various areas of human endeavor, and at some stage it could combine these criteria to constitute perfor- mance indicators of complex systems, such as the community. Work on this is still in the beginning stages; at this point it is more in the nature of theoretical treatises or case studies and models rather than actual instruments of measurement.

While acknowledging that our own attempt to measure community functioning falls far short of the goals of cross- discipline community research or those of the social-indicators approach, it is necessary to stress some of the advantages of the method developed here. It should be remembered, first of all, that the Community Functioning Scale is designed primarily for the use of the social-work and social-welfare practitioner, and that the chief concern of that field of practice is the con- sumer. Given these foci, the objective has been to develop an index that sensitively and comprehensively reflects the state of community health and well-being. It is obviously impossible to mount evaluative studies of every community system that is potentially relevant for the welfare of the population. As an

alternative this writer chose to study the attitudes of the consumers of services, assessing the opinions that were expressed
on their adequacy or inadequacy and the consequent need or
lack of it for services, facilities, and resources.

Some respondents have no knowledge about the quality of
community resources. This may be seen as a drawback to this
method of evaluation, but the questionnaire has sought to
guard against this by providing the option of a "don't know"
response. It may be contended that an individual might lack
good judgment regarding the quality of services, but the co-
gency of this argument is open to doubt. As consumers, or
members of a primary group of consumers, there is nothing
irrelevant in the way they respond to services or to the lack of
services. If they do not have knowledge about what is ulti-
mately best for them or their families, friends, and neighbors,
it is the community's responsibility to enlighten them with
expert knowledge, if such is indeed available. The chances are
that on many, if not most, issues the attitudes of those being
served—or not served—is one of the most important sets of
data that can be gathered for the purpose of judging the quality
of services and resources.

In the final analysis, the worth of the Community Functioning Scale is to be judged (aside from its reliability and validity,
which are methodological considerations) by the degree of sen-
sitivity with which it mirrors a social situation that must
concern planners and practitioners alike. The present instrument is organized as to levels of need and the priorities of areas
of service, so that the subject of community resources can be
dealt with from these two perspectives.

This writer is able to report on the use of the Community
Functioning Scale in one cross-national study devoted to studying the relationship between family functioning and the urban
conditions in Newark, New Jersey, and Melbourne, Australia
(Geismar and Geismar). This research was designed among
others to relate community functioning as measured here to a

variety of social indexes including social status, ethnicity, and degree of family malfunctioning.

Of particular interest for purposes of this presentation is the comparison between a sample of Newark and Melbourne families with regard to response alternative (1) of the Community Functioning Scale, i.e., their expressing satisfaction (find services adequate as they are, or not needed) with services, resources, and opportunities. The findings are summarized in Table 2.

The results supplement a comparison of the two cities on a variety of socioeconomic indexes that reveal Melbourne to be the less problem-ridden community by most indexes of urban well-being available to the investigators. Melbourne families, although predominantly critical of services, are yet twice as affirmative as Newark residents, and the overall difference is consistent with regard to all components of community functioning. The gap in expressed satisfaction is smallest in housing, where Melbournites encountered in 1975 a steep rise in the cost of real estate, and largest in social participation and recreation, which in the American data reflects the lack of safe parks and playgrounds.

In both communities respondents were much more critical of Primary than Secondary Provisions for services and resources—and this was true of a smaller New Jersey community, New Brunswick (see Table 1) as well. It seems that residents of modern, urban communities simply have higher expectations regarding the meeting of basic needs as compared to needs seen as less essential to survival. These findings suggest regularities among industrialized societies in the way needs of urban settlers are being met. However, the relative saliency among needs in the aforementioned cities is at this stage no more than a hypothesis that needs to be tested with a representative sample of urban communities. The noteworthy aspect of the cross-cultural comparison is the demonstration of significance beyond national boundaries of the formulations regard-

Table 2 PERCENTAGE OF RESPONDENTS EXPRESSING
SATISFACTION WITH SERVICES, RESOURCES, AND OPPORTUNITIES
MELBOURNE AND NEWARK COMPARED*

Areas of Service	Melbourne Families	Newark Families	No. of Items in Category
Primary Provisions — Mean Percentage	25.0	12.6	24
Income, Employment and Social Security	31.0	14.6	6
Housing	12.4	11.6	2
Basic Socialization	16.4	8.7	3
Health	42.6	18.2	3
Social Adjustment	21.1	10.0	10
Secondary Provisions — Mean Percentage	42.7	20.7	15
Social Control**	39.5	15.9	4
Social Participation and Recreation	26.7	8.3	2
Secondary Socialization***	50.2	27.7	4
Derived Instrumental Needs****	45.8	31.1	5
Total Mean of Satisfaction	31.8	16.2	39

*There are small variations in the number of items per area in the two studies, as a result of five services having been added in the Melbourne study.
**Includes legal and police protection and political freedom.
***Includes adult- and higher-education and cultural opportunities.
****Includes garbage collection, sewage, public transportation, road maintenance, clean air and water.

Source: Geismar and Geismar. *Families in an Urban Mold.* Reproduced with permission of Pergamon Press.

ing provisions to meet the health-and-welfare need of local populations.

A pretest preceding the study led to only minor adjustment in the wording of a few items (translating the issues of certain American services and resources into their Australian equivalents). The interviewees in both cultures appeared to be responding to issues that touched on the well-being of their respective communities and that were of concern to them. Modifications in wording and the addition of five items, spread over nine areas of service, resources, and opportunities left the conceptual groupings intact.

Following the collection of the community-functioning responses from the Melbourne sample, we subjected the data to factor analysis as a way of determining the empirical clustering or factors among the forty-one items of the scale used in the Australian study.

The principal-component method (using orthogonal rotation of factors and varimax solution) yielded five factors with Eigenvalues of 9.293, 2.047, 1.707, 1.223, and 1.108, respectively. By selecting loadings that were statistically significant and of a magnitude of ≥ 0.30, we were able to utilize thirty-eight out of the forty-one variables. Two items, *services at infant-welfare centers*[19] and *opportunities for religious expression,* received loadings that fell slightly short of the 0.30 cut-off point. The item *schools for children at the elementary and high-school levels* had a statistically significant loading 0.50 under a factor (Instrumental Provisions) that, to the researcher, seemed theoretically irrelevant. The five factors of community functioning, their respective variables, and factor loadings are shown in Table 3.

In interpreting the factor groupings it should be remembered that the Australian version of the questionnaire contained, as

---

19. This appeared as a separate item only in the Australian questionnaire because of the saliency of that service in Melbourne.

stated above, minor changes in the content as well as the wording of items. Furthermore, it is well to keep in mind that the Australian factor structure reflects a cultural perspective that can be expected to differ from an American one simply because of the differences found between the two societies in attitudes toward community services, resources, and opportunities (Geismar and Geismar, Chapter 8).

While the factor loadings of most items are only moderately high, the nature of the variable clusterings and the general absence of multiple factor loadings reveal a definite factor structure that resembles our conceptual classification of the questionnaire items. By and large, a distinction was maintained, allowing for some overlap mainly in Factor V, between Type A Primary Provisions, meeting survival needs, and Type B Secondary Provisions, pertaining to needs with a lesser degree of urgency.

Factor I groups together mainly Type A resources for the socially handicapped and deviant, which parallel rather closely our social-adjustment category. Factor V, likewise, comprises mainly Type A provisions, whose common denominator is economic security. Exclusively Type B provisions are represented by Factor II, encompassing resources for meeting social, political, and cultural needs, and Factor III, bringing together instrumental services and resources. Only Factor IV is clearly split between Type A and B provisions. Its interpretation—services and resources for a job, home, and leisure—may, indeed, represent an aspiration characteristic of Australian society, which is strongly family oriented and tends to view work, home, and leisure as a collective goal for its citizens.

Factor analysis has, therefore, led to a diminution of theoretically derived subcategories, reducing eleven such groupings to five factors whose common conceptual denominators were partly similar to and partly different from the original categorizations. On the whole, the integrity between Primary and Secondary Provisions for meeting needs was maintained.

Table 3   COMMUNITY FUNCTIONING FACTORS, VARIABLES,
AND FACTOR LOADINGS

Factor I   *Provisions for the Socially Handicapped,*
Deviant, and Minorities

Special classes for children	.43
Job training for those lacking skills	.34
Counseling and guidance	.40
Treatment for addicted and maladjusted	.50
Child placement away from home	.69
Nursing homes for the elderly	.54
Leisure service for the elderly	.50
Care for physically handicapped	.76
Care for the mentally handicapped	.75
Home services for the handicapped	.34
Parole, probation for youth and adults	.60
Acceptance of all including minorities	.44

Factor II   *Provisions for Political, Social, and*
Cultural Opportunities

Opportunities for political expression	.44
Opportunities for social change	.46
Provisions for postsecondary education	.59
Adult education and programs	.66
Cultural and artistic opportunities	.59

Factor III   *Provisions for Instrumental Services*

Protection against personal damage with aid of fire and police departments	.43
Transportation to work and shopping	.52
Shopping within easy reach	.37
Garbage and sewage services	.64
Road maintenance and cleaning	.63
Clean air and water	.49

(continued)

Table 3 (continued)

Factor IV   *Provisions for Job, Home, and Leisure*

Job opportunities for all able to work	.71
Job finding and placement	.65
Less costly private housing	.43
Day-care centers for working mothers	.39
Opportunity for economic and social advancement	.34
Social and recreational neighborhood organizations	.32
Sports and recreational facilities	.35

Factor V   *Provisions for Economic Security*

Financial assistance for those in need	.56
Unemployment insurance	.38
Workers' compensation	.69
Old-age pensions	.52
Low-cost public housing	.36
Low-cost medical services	.42
Low-cost dental services	.30
Low-cost legal services	.33

Factor analysis, as applied here to community-functioning data, in ways similar to its application to family-functioning data (see Chapter V, section 7), enables the researcher to validate theoretical (nonempirical) classifications (or reject them if the analysis does not work out) and reduce the number of working dimensions of the research instrument. The Melbourne data analysis, comprising an N of 228, served more as a demonstration of the technique than a processing of a final product for American use. As such, the potential utility of the technique became evident both in its support of the basic conceptual approach and the emergence of simplified structure applicable to statistical measurement. Future use of factor analysis in the study of community functioning is definitely recommended, and its usefulness must be judged in each instance in relation to the research population from which the factor structure was derived.

Factor analysis is, of course, only one of several approaches to the statistical treatment of the community-functioning data. Another possibility is Guttman scaling by using aggregate scores for the eleven subcategories of the Community Functioning Scale. A decision on which statistical technique to use may have to be made after some experimentation aimed at determining the best fit between a given model and a particular set of data.

There remains the long-range issue of demonstrating the utility of the Community Functioning Scale, not only as a valid index of attitudes but as a true indicator of the community's social situation. And with this statement our chain of arguments has come full circle, for in order to prove that community attitudes are indeed good indicators of the way the community functions or meets the diverse needs of its residents, our method of measurement needs to be compared with objective indexes of community functioning, of which the social indicators discussed above are an example. While both approaches tap somewhat different dimensions of community life, a significant intercorrelation is, nonetheless, anticipated—for in the final analysis the present, easily administered measure, like its counterpart, must serve as an index of community well-being and quality of life.

VII. Family and Community Functioning: Some Research Issues

T he joining in one volume of two major concepts, family functioning and community functioning, for purposes of furthering empirical research can be justified by the claim, made in the Introduction, that they are reciprocally relevant concepts. According to the social-systems framework, to which this volume owes a great deal, this interrelationship of concepts is inherent in the fact that the family is a system that generally operates within the community system. Given this observation, a number of others follow: the family is dependent upon the community, and its own social functioning is partly determined by the nature of community functioning. Communities, in turn, are strongly influenced by the structure, attitudes, and behavior of the families in their midst, which constitute one of the most basic social systems they encompass. Substantial changes in either system are bound to have effects upon the other.

It is the latter thesis that has substantial implications for social-work policy and practice. Although the time is probably past when an agency was concerned exclusively with its client and oblivious to the needs and requirements of those persons and systems with which he or she maintained contact (this approach was particularly characteristic of traditional psychotherapy), the present American welfare structure still reveals a predominantly narrow and primary client-focused pattern of service.

This is not the place to enumerate the many reasons for this individualized and fragmented social-welfare picture. It is sufficient to say that efforts at integration would be aided substantially by methods that would permit the assessment of needs and the exploration of problems of client systems that are reciprocally related, such as family and community. Neither family treatment nor community planning and organization can be practiced effectively without an awareness of and reference to each other. Service to families is heavily dependent upon the resources and facilities furnished by the community, while strategies of community organization are guided in part by the nature of family life within the community's boundaries. Changes in one are bound to have far-reaching implications for the other. Widespread unemployment, for example, will affect local consumption patterns, taxes, job-training programs, rehabilitation and financial assistance resources, and a host of other factors. An increase in family disorganization, whether due to delinquency, drug abuse, out-of-wedlock births, or economic strains, has a great deal of impact on the community's welfare budget, its social services and correctional system, and perhaps on the manner in which priorities for the future will be ordered.

Despite this intertwining of influences emanating from the family and community, the relationship between their levels of functioning is anything but simple, as evidenced from a recent comparative study (Geismar and Geismar). Of course, a distinction must be made between the use of both scales as aggregate measures, applying to total communities or neighborhoods, and their use as indicators of individual attitudes and performance.

With reference to the former, common sense would suggest that the social functioning of families mirrors the functioning of the social system in which they live as measured by the degree of affirmation expressed by its residents in the services, resources, and opportunities. This postulation is based on an assumption, underlying the juxtaposition of topics in this book, that in industrial society family and community life are interdependent and affect each other over time. The last phrase, "over time," is rather crucial, however, in sustaining this argument. One can think of a number of variables that modify the assumed interdependence of family and community functioning. One of them is the time factor. New residents, especially those coming from different cultures, may not have had an opportunity to interact with the community in which they live. Their family life may, in fact, reflect past experiences and conditions and be insulated from activities of the local community. Continued residence is likely to lead to the kind of interdependence referred to above.

Other factors that might intervene between the postulated relationship of family and community functioning are: 1) cultural remoteness, not related to brief residence, creating a degree of autonomy that reduces the need for reliance on the community; and 2) highly privileged position, which permits a

degree of independence made possible only by personal resources. The latter will permit a purchase of services, wherever
these may be available, and reduce the need for reliance on the
community.

Determining the nature of the relationship between family
and community functioning as aggregate measures calls for a
test of this relationship in a sample of communities. Research
by this writer on the subject has up to this point yielded only a
comparison of two settings: 1) two municipalities within
Greater Melbourne, Australia; and 2) Newark, New Jersey.
These data showed that the much greater affirmation by Melbourne residents of their community resources was matched by
a lesser prevalence of family malfunctioning (Geismar and
Geismar, Chapters 5 and 8). Because of the small number of
cases involved and the absence of matching on potentially
intervening variables, these findings are at best suggestive of
empirical support for the thesis on the relationship between
the aggregate measures of community and family functioning.

With regard to the relationship between family functioning
and attitudes toward community services as personal attrib-
utes rather than group characteristics, one would also predict a
direct association between these variables. The argument here
hinges on the notion that people with many problems tend to
blame, often with good reason, elements in the environment for
their predicament. Hence, individuals whose family life is
characterized by various types of malfunctioning would tend to
take a more jaundiced view of the services in the community
than persons without such troubles.

This thesis received substantial support in our Newark data,
but not the Melbourne ones (Geismar and Geismar, Chapter 8),
which showed no relationship between family functioning and
attitudes toward services, resources, and opportunities in the
two communities. Those New Jersey residents with proportionately more inter- and intrapersonal and environmental
problems when compared with their less problematic confreres,

were more prone to question the efficacy of the social-welfare structure because of their seemingly more negative experience with community resources. The more problematically functioning Australians were not equally turned off by their services.

The relationship between social status and attitudes toward community services roughly parallels the above findings (for details see Geismar and Geismar, Chapter 8), giving additional support to the contention that it is not problem function *per se*—which is roughly comparable in the two countries—but the experience with the services and resources that determines the family-community functioning relationship.

A further issue for research, but one not addressed by prior studies, is the relationship between the autonomy of community services and resources and family functioning. More specifically, the question is posed whether as a result of optimum opportunity for local policy making and power to change things, services tend to be more responsive to family need and in this way enhance social functioning. Any inquiry seeking answers to this question would have to control for the effect of such intervening variables as economic situation, social stratification of the population, and the general quality of services, including the system for delivering them.

We contend here that while the issue of community autonomy rests on a number of considerations, including the value of local self-determination and people's wish to exercise power, information about family functioning as a dependent variable carries with it the compelling argument that it is at the heart of community well-being and can be objectively measured as we have sought to demonstrate here. Autonomy as the independent variable does, of course, require an operational definition that takes into account not merely a community's ability to decide for itself but also the degree of community participation at the levels of policy making, service monitoring, and service evaluation.

Community planners will be interested to learn how changes

over time in the community's service system as gauged by input measures, such as budget, quantity and variety of services available, etc., and output measures, such as our scale of community functioning, are related to changes in family functioning. With reference to the latter, a useful distinction might be made between expressive and instrumental functioning. A tenable hypothesis would postulate a chain reaction in which services first affect instrumental family behavior and that, in turn, influences the nature of functioning in the intra- and extrafamilial relationship areas. It is asserted, then, that improved community services affect expressive family functioning indirectly by their positive impact on instrumental family behavior.

The relationship over time between expressive and instrumental family functioning is not well researched. In one study, where a clinical and predominantly lower-class population was investigated, the inference was drawn that problems in the expressive areas precede malfunctioning in instrumental behavior (Geismar 1964). Results of another study on the interrelationship of family problems "contradicted the assumption that economic problems of families are related to personal ones and also the clinical assumption that interpersonal problems in the marital and parental roles are closely related" (Brim, Fairchild, and Borgatta). On the other hand, Blood and Wolfe found marital satisfaction positively related to social status (pp. 253-255), while this writer found a strong direct correlation between social status and family functioning among young urban families (Geismar 1973, pp. 54-67). A further study of a clinical population also found that practical difficulties, interpersonal conflict, and personal defects and maladjustment were significantly interrelated (Krupinski, Marshall, and Yule). None of these studies examined the relationships among types of functioning from the perspective of change over time, however.

Those who are interested in planning community strategies

that attempt to strengthen family life will be interested in verifying or disproving the above hypothesis, for support of the hypothesis would suggest that high priority be given to improving health and welfare services at the community level.

For researchers and administrators interested in programs of intervention designed to help improve the social functioning of deprived families, the nature of the community services and resources that can bolster or impede such a program are an important consideration. A plausible hypothesis would postulate that the success of such programs of intervention is directly related to the quality of the relevant community resources.

This hypothesis is in need of testing by reviewing the outcome of such projects in relation to the services, resources, and facilities that exist at the community level. At least one study, whose goal was the prevention of family disorganization, gave evidence that poor resources were an inhibiting factor in the attainment of action objectives (Geismar, Lagay, et al., p. 70ff.). Since so many antipoverty projects mushroomed in the wake of the 1964 declaration of War on Poverty, this thesis of the interrelationship between the quality of appropriate services and an improvement in the social functioning of the poor would be of great interest, but it has received little systematic attention. Project after project has been conducted under some organization's favorite slogan or banner: the poor need more job training or better health services or cheaper transportation or more participation in decision making. There followed inevitably a demonstration project designed to meet one or the other of the projected and probably accurately assessed needs. But the results, if known—and more often than not they did not become known—were generally no change or insignificant change in the social functioning of the poor. These projects have paid scant attention to the many interrelated problems and needs of the target populations or to the role of the community's service system in supporting or hampering the attainment of project objectives.

The latter hypothesis touches upon a key consideration in the mobilizing of any effort aimed at modifying the social conditions of individuals and groups. Medicine and psychiatrists have long paid lip service to the needs of the total person and the total family but family medicine and family psychiatry are slow to emerge as full-fledged operational disciplines, indicating that an awareness of the problem is not necessarily tantamount to institutional change. The other social helping professions, particularly social work, have borrowed heavily from social-science theory, which stresses the systems approach, but it is much more emphasized in professional writings than in professional practice.

One of the preconditions for translating a seemingly promising approach into institutional forms is the availabilty of tools. Such tools would permit the practitioner to begin with an assessment of conditions and delineation of problems affecting the total individual, group, or system. After all, the planning and rendering of services must necessarily be firmly based on such a prior assessment. The two instruments that we have presented here to evaluate the social functioning of families and communities do not cover—let alone exhaust—the need for such research implements in this area. Although one hopes the two scales will prove useful to the researcher and practitioner, they are above all an illustration of that which can be done in shifting professional action from tradition, insight, and practice wisdom to objective knowledge and tested theory.

Appendix A:
Self-Evaluation of Change
in Family Functioning

SELF-EVALUATION OF CHANGE IN FAMILY FUNCTIONING*

As part of our study of families who have received services, we would like to find out how you think things have changed for you and your family between the time when services were started and when they were terminated (or up to the present, if services are continuing). Please indicate in every area by a circle whether a change occurred in your situation, and if so, how much of a change. If you don't know the answer to the question, or if it is not relevant, circle "Don't Know" or "Not Relevant," whichever is appropriate.

THE SITUATION NOW IS

	(1) Much Worse	(2) Slightly Worse	(3) No Change	(4) Slightly Better	(5) Much Better	(0) Don't Know	Not Relevant
A.1. 7. How do you and your husband (wife) get along generally?	W	w	Nc	b	B	?	Nr
8. Has there been any change in how you and your husband (wife) put up with each other's moods?	W	w	Nc	b	B	?	Nr
9. Any change in how you and your husband (wife) discuss problems and share feelings?	W	w	Nc	b	B	?	Nr
10. Any change in how you get along sexually?	W	w	Nc	b	B	?	Nr

*I am indebted to Dr. Ursula Gerhart for constructing this client questionnaire, which corresponds to the categories of the St. Paul Scale of Family Functioning.

(continued)

THE SITUATION NOW IS

	(1) Much Worse	(2) Slightly Worse	(3) No Change	(4) Slightly Better	(5) Much Better	(0) Don't Know	Not Relevant
11. Any change in the way you and your husband (wife) feel about each other's leisure time activities?	W	w	Nc	b	B	?	Nr
2. 12. How do you and your husband (wife) get along with your children?	W	w	Nc	b	B	?	Nr
13. Has there been a change in how you feel about your children?	W	w	Nc	b	B	?	Nr
3. 14. How do the children in your home get along with each other?	W	w	Nc	b	B	?	Nr
4. 15. Has there been any change in how you and your husband (wife) plan for the future?	W	w	Nc	b	B	?	Nr
16. Any change in how you, as a family, do things together?	W	w	Nc	b	B	?	Nr
17. Any change in how you, as a family, "pull together" in times of trouble?	W	w	Nc	b	B	?	Nr

Appendix A

247

THE SITUATION NOW IS

	(1) Much Worse	(2) Slightly Worse	(3) No Change	(4) Slightly Better	(5) Much Better	(0) Don't Know	Not Relevant
5. 18. If someone other than your husband (wife), children, or your parents live with you, has there been any change in how all of you have been getting along together?	W	w	Nc	b	B	?	Nr
B.1. 19. Has there been any change in how you feel about yourself?	W	w	Nc	b	B	?	Nr
20. Do you feel that your dress and general appearance have changed since we first saw you?	W	w	Nc	b	B	?	Nr
21. Has there been any change in how you get along with people in general?	W	w	Nc	b	B	?	Nr
22. Do you think there has been any change in how your husband (wife) feels about himself (herself) and gets along with people in general?	W	w	Nc	b	B	?	Nr
C.1. 23. Has there been any change in the condition and amount of your children's clothing?	W	w	Nc	b	B	?	Nr

THE SITUATION NOW IS

	(1) Much Worse	(2) Slightly Worse	(3) No Change	(4) Slightly Better	(5) Much Better	(0) Don't Know	Not Relevant
24. Any change in how you feed and generally take care of your children?	W	w	Nc	b	B	?	Nr
2. 25. Any change in how you and your husband (wife) agree on disciplining the children?	W	w	Nc	b	B	?	Nr
26. Any change in the way you actually discipline the children?	W	w	Nc	b	B	?	Nr
D.1. 27. Has there been a change in how you get along with your family and your husband's (wife's) family?	W	w	Nc	b	B	?	Nr
28. Has anything changed in how you get along with your neighbors?	W	w	Nc	b	B	?	Nr
29. Any change in satisfaction with the way you spend your free time?	W	w	Nc	b	B	?	Nr

THE SITUATION NOW IS

		(1) Much Worse	(2) Slightly Worse	(3) No Change	(4) Slightly Better	(5) Much Better	(0) Don't Know	Not Relevant
2.	30. Has there been any change in the way you and your husband participate in clubs, unions, unions, and other organizations?	W	w	Nc	b	B	?	Nr
	31. Any change in how you or your husband (wife) feel about belonging to clubs and other organizations?	W	w	Nc	b	B	?	Nr
E.1.	32. Since services started, what changes have there been in your actual cash income?	W	w	Nc	b	B	?	Nr
	33. How satisfied are you with your present income as compared to the way you felt about your income when services started?	W	w	Nc	b	B	?	Nr
	34. How does your present income, compared to previous income, meet your actual needs?	W	w	Nc	b	B	?	Nr

THE SITUATION NOW IS

		(1) Much Worse	(2) Slightly Worse	(3) No Change	(4) Slightly Better	(5) Much Better	(0) Don't Know	Not Relevant
2.	35. If you, or your husband (wife) are employed, has there been a change in job satisfaction?	W	w	Nc	b	B	?	Nr
	36. Is that job more suited to you or your husband's (wife's) abilities than before?	W	w	Nc	b	B	?	Nr
3.	37. Has there been a change in how you and your husband (wife) agree on how money ought to be spent?	W	w	Nc	b	B	?	Nr
	38. If you have any debts, is there any change in how you are able to meet payment on these debts?	W	w	Nc	b	B	?	Nr
	39. What kind of money managers or budgeters are you now as compared to then?	W	w	Nc	b	B	?	Nr
F.1.	40. Any change in the kind of apartment or house that you now occupy?	W	w	Nc	b	B	?	Nr

THE SITUATION NOW IS

	(1) Much Worse	(2) Slightly Worse	(3) No Change	(4) Slightly Better	(5) Much Better	(0) Don't Know	Not Relevant
41. Is the neighborhood you live in better or worse now?	W	w	Nc	b	B	?	Nr
42. Has there been a change in the quantity or quality of your household furniture and furnishings?	W	w	Nc	b	B	?	Nr
2. 43. Has there been a change in your (or your spouse's) housekeeping habits?	W	w	Nc	b	B	?	Nr
44. Have you changed in the way you (or your spouse) serve and plan meals?	W	w	Nc	b	B	?	Nr
45. Has there been a change in the ease with which you (or your spouse) perform your household chores?	W	w	Nc	b	B	?	Nr
G.1. 46. How is your health and that of members of your immediate family now as compared to the time services began?	W	w	Nc	b	B	?	Nr

THE SITUATION NOW IS

		(1) Much Worse	(2) Slightly Worse	(3) No Change	(4) Slightly Better	(5) Much Better	(0) Don't Know	Not Relevant
2.	47. Have there been changes in the way you take care of your own and your family's health needs?	W	w	Nc	b	B	?	Nr
	48. Any change in the manner in which you get medical and dental checkups or keep appointments?	W	w	Nc	b	B	?	Nr
H.1.	49. Has there been any change in your feeling about the social worker who has been serving you?	W	w	Nc	b	B	?	Nr
	50. Has there been any change in the way you are able to work together with your social worker?	W	w	Nc	b	B	?	Nr
I.1.	51. Has there been a change in how you feel about schools and education for your children?	W	w	Nc	b	B	?	Nr

THE SITUATION NOW IS

	(1) Much Worse	(2) Slightly Worse	(3) No Change	(4) Slightly Better	(5) Much Better	(0) Don't Know	Not Relevant
2. 52. Has there been any change in your church- or synagogue-going habits?	W	w	Nc	b	B	?	Nr
3. 53. Are there any changes in the way you use health resources, such as clinics, private doctors, hospitals?	W	w	Nc	b	B	?	Nr
4. 54. How do you now use social agencies, as compared to when services started?	W	w	Nc	b	B	?	Nr
5. 55. Has there been a change in how you use recreational agencies?	W	w	Nc	b	B	?	Nr

Appendix B:
Documenting and Rating
the Individual Behavior
and Adjustment of Children*

*I acknowledge gratefully the contributions of Isabel Wolock, who adapted the framework of the St. Paul Scale to the measurement in greater depth of the social functioning of children.

GUIDELINES TO A PROFILE ON CHILD FUNCTIONING

1. Health and Health Practices

    —Diseases, handicaps?
    —Treatment sought? Medical instructions followed?
    —Disease-prevention and dental-hygiene practices observed? (sanitation, diet)
    —Height, Weight

2. Source and Use of Money

    (A) Obtaining Money
       —Allowance? Is it adequate? regular? in line with family finances?
       —If old enough and needs money will the child earn extra money by working part-time and/or doing extra household chores?
       —Does child steal, falsify expenses?
       —Does child borrow money? often? Does child repay money?

    (B) Use of Money
       —Does child use money for anti-social and/or self-destructive activities? (drugs, alcohol)
       —Do expenditures exceed amount available?
       —Does child save money?
       —Does child plan expenditures?

3. Role Performance as Peer

    —Does child have many friends? show continuity in peer relationships? maintain friends for long periods of time? participate satisfactorily in peer groups? exploit friends or permit exploitation of self by friends?
    —Is child in conflict with peers?

—Associate with groups whose behavior is not acceptable to immediate community?
—Participate with others in delinquent acts?

4. Role Performance as Citizen

—Does child show consideration for persons and property outside the home? or express disrespect for persons and property outside the home by engaging in rude or assaulting behavior, destruction of property?
—Does child show respect for laws and legal authority? or express disrespect for laws and legal authority by engaging in illegal acts?
—Does child have aspirations for a socially acceptable career goal?
—Is the child a member of one or more formally organized clubs, associations, etc.?

5. Role Performance as Child

—Does child get along well with family members? or behave violently, destructively, deceitfully, or assaultively against family members?
—Does child create severe conflict within family which threatens the family unit?
—Does child perform expected and appropriate household duties?
—Does child assume responsibility for grooming, cleanliness, and personal hygiene?
—Does child accept appropriate discipline and guidance?
—Does child meet most of appropriate parental expectations?

6. Role Performance as Sibling

—Does child exhibit positive emotional ties and mutual identification with other children?
—Does child play with siblings, share playthings, enjoy siblings' company, take pride in achievements of siblings?

—Does child fight frequently with other children? initiate or receive frequent teasing, bullying, or other emotional cruelty?
—Is conflict between child and siblings so severe that physical violence results that warrants intervention? or is fighting and bickering normal for age?
—Is sibling rivalry excessive or normal?

7. Role Performance as Pupil

—Attendance regular? or excessive truancy?
—Positive attitude toward school and learning?
—Does child "act out"? Does child disobey school regulations (resulting in suspension, expulsion)?
—Does school work up to approximate ability?
—Does child complete assignments? Are grades poor or good?
—Does child experience so much failure and frustration that removal from school is being considered?
—Does child participate in extracurricular activities?

8. Intellectual State

—Does child perform up to mental capacity? or below?
—Is child mentally retarded? Does child receive special training?
—Does child's mental defectiveness require that the child receive institutional training or custodial care? Is such care provided?

9. Emotional State

—Does child's emotional health appear good? Has child a positive self-image? Does child relate well to others? Is he/she satisfied with his/her life? Does child show evidence of ability to cope with new situations?
—Does child receive treatment for emotional disorder? Do emotional problems impair social functioning?
—Does child's mental illness require hospitalization?
—Is child excessively withdrawn? or does other behavior suggest disturbance or serious problems in relating to others?
—Results of psychological testing?

10. Relationship with Parents

—Does child get along well with parents?
—Or is conflict with parents so considerable that separation is considered desirable by child, parent, and/or agency?
—Does child feel secure, accepted in relationship with parents?
—Can child express and demonstrate warmth and affection when appropriate?
—Does child have positive feelings and respect for parents?

11. Relationship with Agency

—Does child show willingness to engage in agency program? cooperate with agency personnel, recognize and/or deal with problems he/she faces?
—Does child keep appointments, make appropriate use of agency personnel?
—Or does child manipulate agency workers, play one against the other?
—Does child display physical violence or verbal assault and other types of insulting behavior?

GUIDELINE TO RATING DEVELOPMENT AND
INDIVIDUAL BEHAVIOR AND ADJUSTMENT
OF CHILD SERVED

Notes on Using Guideline

Whenever a child is a client of the agency his or her behavior will be rated individually using this guideline. Other children will be dealt with collectively as instructed in the general guidelines.

Since the children range from infants to almost adulthood, the criteria contained in these guidelines vary in their applicability. Use your judgment in applying the criteria. Use only if appropriate.

In making a decision about a particular rating consider both the expressed and underlying satisfaction of the child with a particular role or situation.

1. HEALTH AND HEALTH PRACTICES

INADEQUATE	MARGINAL	ADEQUATE
Child has disease that endangers public health; no measures taken for isolation or treatment. Other serious health conditions or handicaps for which proper care is not provided.

Proper treatment or quarantine not secured for disease endangering life of person and/or public health. Parents or parent surrogates neglect or refuse to provide medical care for health and well-being of children. Disease prevention practices (sanitation, diet, etc.) not followed. Conditions so poor that physical neglect of child is involved. | Presence of chronic or major physical disease or handicap receiving some treatment, but permits minimal functioning.

Refusal or failure to get or continue medical care for minor ailments. Medical instructions disregarded or not followed consistently. Disease prevention practices not generally followed. | Disease or handicaps, if present, are receiving appropriate care with resulting favorable adjustment.

Concern shown about ill health or handicaps. Medical care promptly sought when needed; medical instructions followed.

Disease-prevention and dental-hygiene practices observed. |

2. SOURCE AND USE OF MONEY
(Code only if appropriate, i.e., child old enough to receive money [allowance] and spend for certain of own expenses.)

INADEQUATE	MARGINAL	ADEQUATE
a. *Obtaining Money*		
Child is completely deprived of financial resources for necessary expenditures—clothing,	Child receives barely enough money or allowance for expenses; or on irregular basis,	Child receives sufficient money—not excessive nor too little—to meet expenditures. Allowance

INADEQUATE	MARGINAL	ADEQUATE
recreational, leisure activities, and other needs—even though family finances adequate. If old enough and needs money, makes no attempt to earn money by working part-time and/or doing extra household chores.	even though family finances adequate. If old enough and capable, rarely will attempt to earn extra money if needed by doing part-time work or additional household chores, etc.	or money paid on regular basis. If old enough and capable, when in need of money attempts to earn by part-time work, doing extra household chores, etc.
Obtains money by stealing, falsifying expenses, etc.	Borrows frequently from others, only occasionally repays.	Only occasionally asks for additional money from parents or parent surrogate.
Borrows frequently from others; almost never repays.		May borrow on occasion but repays money promptly.
		Amount received in line with general family finances.

b. *Use of Money*

INADEQUATE	MARGINAL	ADEQUATE
Uses money regularly for anti-social and/or self-destructive activities—drugs, alcohol, etc.	Expenditures considerably exceed amount available. Never saves money. Spending done without any planning.	Expenditures generally within amount of money available. Does manage to save occasionally. Plans expenditures.

3.   ROLE PERFORMANCE AS PEER

INADEQUATE	MARGINAL	ADEQUATE
Participation with others in delinquent acts. Inability to relate to peers suggests severe emotional disturbance.	Has few friends, is in conflict with peers or associates with groups whose behavior is not acceptable to immediate community.	Is well liked, has friends, participates satisfactorily in peer groups. Shows continuity in peer relationships, tends to maintain

INADEQUATE	MARGINAL	ADEQUATE
Often involved in severe conflicts with peers.	Absence of continuity in friendships. Keeps friends for only short periods of time. Excessive exploitation of friends or permits excessive exploitation of self by friends.	friends for longer periods of time. Exploitation of or by friends minimal.

4. ROLE PERFORMANCE AS CITIZEN

Expresses and acts out feelings of considerable disrespect for persons and property outside home by engaging in rude or assaultive behavior, destruction of property; shows general disrespect for persons and property. Expresses and acts out lack of respect for laws and legal authority by engaging in illegal acts of various kinds.	Expresses but only infrequently acts out disrespect for persons and property outside of home. Expresses but only infrequently acts out disrespect for laws and legal authority.	Generally shows consideration for persons and property outside the home. Generally shows respect for laws and legal authority. Has aspirations for socially acceptable career goal. Is a member of one or more formally organized clubs, associations, centers, etc.

5. ROLE PERFORMANCE AS CHILD

Violent, destructive, deceitful, or assaultive behavior against family members. Creates severe conflict within family which threatens family units.	Gets along poorly with family members. Rarely performs household duties. Fails to assume responsibility for grooming,	Gets along well with family members. Performs expected and appropriate household duties.

INADEQUATE	MARGINAL	ADEQUATE
	cleanliness, and personal hygiene. Inability to accept appropriate discipline and guidance. Fails generally to meet most of appropriate parental expectations.	Assumes responsibility for grooming, cleanliness, and personal hygiene. Evidence of ability to accept appropriate discipline and guidance. For the most part meets most of appropriate parental expectations.

6. ROLE PERFORMANCE AS SIBLING

INADEQUATE	MARGINAL	ADEQUATE
Conflict between child and siblings is so severe that it results in physical violence or cruelty that warrants intervention.	Emotional ties with other children in family weak. Rarely plays with other children. Fights frequently with other children. Is either the recipient or initiator of frequent teasing, bullying, or other emotional or physical cruelty. Rarely shares, shows little loyalty to other children in family or pride in other's achievements. Excessive sibling rivalry present.	Positive emotional ties and mutual identification with other children in family. Depending on age, often plays with sibling(s), shares playthings with siblings, enjoys siblings' company, takes pride in achievements of siblings. Fighting and bickering normal for age. Normal degree of sibling rivalry present.

7. ROLE PERFORMANCE AS PUPIL

INADEQUATE	MARGINAL	ADEQUATE
Excessive truancy, disruptiveness, incorrigibility, property destruction necessitating intervention. Other infringements of school regulations resulting in suspension, expulsion.	Acting-out or withdrawn behavior of less serious nature. Attendance not regular but no action taken. Little positive feeling toward school.	Attends regularly, school work approximates ability, positive attitude toward school and learning. Acting out limited to occasional pranks.
Child experiences so much failure and frustration that removal from school is being considered.	Performance considerably below ability level. Shown inconsistent failure to complete assignments, poor grades, etc.	At least minimal participation in extracurricular activities. Cooperative attitude toward supplementary instruction when offered.

8. INTELLECTUAL STATE

Mental defectiveness requiring institutional training or custodial care that is not provided.	Performance below mental capacity. Mental retardation severely limits functioning, but special training, such as special class, received.	Performs up to mental capacity.
	Child not retarded, but performs well below capacity.	

9. EMOTIONAL STATE

Mental illness requiring intervention or resulting in hospitalization. Excessively withdrawn	Emotional disorder evident but receiving treatment or not serious enough to justify inter-	Emotional health appears good, has positive self-image, enjoys appropriate activities, re-

Inadequate	Marginal	Adequate
or other behavior suggesting disturbance or serious problems in relating to others.	vention; little personal satisfaction experienced in life.	lates well to others, is satisfied with his/her life.
Tests indicate serious emotional problems.	Tests indicate mild emotional disturbance.	Shows evidence of ability to cope with new situations.
Emotional problems seriously interfere with functioning.	Evidence that emotional problems impair social functioning.	

10. RELATIONSHIP WITH PARENTS

Inadequate	Marginal	Adequate
Relationship with parents characterized by so much conflict and/or tension that separation is considered desirable by child, parent, and/or agency.	Has a poor relationship with parent or parents. Conflict considerable but not to point where separation considered as solution to problems.	Gets along well with parents or parent surrogate. Conflict minimal.
Complete absence of positive feeling for parent or parent surrogate.	Unable to express any degree of warmth and affection toward parents or parent surrogate.	Feels secure, accepted in relationship with parent(s) or parent surrogate(s).
	Evidence of strong feeling of insecurity in relationship with parent(s) or parent surrogate(s).	Evidence of ability to express and demonstrate warmth and affection when appropriate.
	Little respect or positive feelings for parents.	Have overall positive feeling and respect for parent(s) or parent surrogate(s).

11. RELATIONSHIP WITH AGENCY

Inadequate	Marginal	Adequate
Physical violence or verbal assault and other types of insulting behavior.	Child reluctant to participate in agency program—cooperate with agency personnel	Child shows willingness to engage in agency program and works toward enhancing or im-

INADEQUATE	MARGINAL	ADEQUATE
Absolute refusal to acknowledge any problems.	and to recognize and/or deal with problems he/she faces.	proving social functioning.
Refusal to participate in agency program.	Tends to manipulate various agency workers involved in case; child tends to play one against the other.	Keeps scheduled appointments with worker. Makes appropriate use of various agency personnel.

**Appendix C:
Evaluating the Family's
Social Functioning:
Precoded Schedule**

I.D. Number

1 2 3 4 5

card

Family Relationships and Unity

Marital Relationship (5)

	Almost Always	Often	Sometimes	Rarely or Never	Insuf. Info.	Not Applicable
6. Husband and wife show consideration for one another	4	3	2	1	0	blank
7. Severe conflict between husband and wife	1	2	3	4	0	blank
8. Husband and wife discuss problems and share feelings	4	3	2	1	0	blank
9. Mutually satisfying sexual relationship between husband and wife	4	3	2	1	0	blank
10. Husband and wife share leisure-time activities	4	3	2	1	0	blank

Relationship Between Parents and Children (7)

	Almost Always	Often	Sometimes	Rarely or Never	Insuf. Info.	Not Applicable
11. Parent(s) show(s) favoritism toward child(ren)	1	2	3	4	0	blank

	Almost Always	Often	Sometimes	Rarely or Never	Insuf. Info.	Not Applicable
12. Parent(s) show(s) evidence of warm, affectionate feelings toward child(ren)	4	3	2	1	0	blank
13. Conflict between parent(s) and child(ren)	1	2	3	4	0	blank
14. Children show consideration for parents	4	3	2	1	0	blank
15. Parent(s) show(s) understanding of needs of child(ren)	4	3	2	1	0	blank
16. Children appear to feel secure and have sense of belonging	4	3	2	1	0	blank
17. Parent(s)' anger unpredictable and erratic	1	2	3	4	0	blank
Relationship Among Children (4)						
18. Conflict among children	1	2	3	4	0	blank
19. Children appear to have positive emotional ties to one another	4	3	2	1	0	blank
20. Children show jealousy toward one another	1	2	3	4	0	blank
21. Children show loyalty to one another	4	3	2	1	0	blank

	Almost Always	Often	Sometimes	Rarely or Never	Insuf. Info.	Not Applicable
Family Solidarity (5)						
22. Family members show concern and interest in one another's welfare	4	3	2	1	0	blank
23. Engage in family activities together	4	3	2	1	0	blank
24. Family "pulls together" in times of trouble	4	3	2	1	0	blank
25. Family members share goals and values	4	3	2	1	0	blank
26. Decisions and plans are based on personal gratification of one member rather than family as a whole	1	2	3	4	0	blank
Relationship with other Members of Household (2)*						
27. Presence of other household member* creates conflict and resentment in family	1	2	3	4	0	blank
28. Other members of household help strengthen family unity	4	3	2	1	0	blank

*Refers to any one in household other than member of nuclear family.

Individual Behavior and Adjustment

Father (18)

	Almost Always	Often	Sometimes	Rarely or Never	Insuf. Info.	Not Applicable
29. Has been involved in minor law violations (e.g., traffic violations)	1	2	3	4	0	blank
30. Has been involved in more serious conflicts with the law	1	2	3	4	0	blank
31. Has engaged in deviant social behavior (e.g., drinking, drugs, sexual, etc.)	1	2	3	4	0	blank
32. Appears to have positive self-image	4	3	2	1	0	blank
33. Emotional health appears to be good	4	3	2	1	0	blank
34. Gets along poorly with most people	1	2	3	4	0	blank
35. Is concerned about appearance	4	3	2	1	0	blank
36. Intellectual functioning appears to be at average or above average level	4	3	2	1	0	blank
Performs well as:						
37. spouse	4	3	2	1	0	blank
38. homemaker or helper	4	3	2	1	0	blank
39. parent	4	3	2	1	0	blank
40. wage earner	4	3	2	1	0	blank
41. member of community	4	3	2	1	0	blank

	Almost Always	Often	Sometimes	Rarely or Never	Insuf. Info.	Not Applicable
Derives satisfaction from being:						
42. spouse	4	3	2	1	0	blank
43. homemaker or helper	4	3	2	1	0	blank
44. parent	4	3	2	1	0	blank
45. wage earner	4	3	2	1	0	blank
46. member of community	4	3	2	1	0	blank
Mother (18)						
47. Has been involved in minor law violations (e.g., traffic violations)	1	2	3	4	0	blank
48. Has been involved in more serious conflicts with the law	1	2	3	4	0	blank
49. Has engaged in deviant social behavior (e.g., drinking, drugs, sexual, etc.)	1	2	3	4	0	blank
50. Appears to have positive self-image	4	3	2	1	0	blank
51. Emotional health appears to be good	4	3	2	1	0	blank
52. Gets along poorly with most people	1	2	3	4	0	blank
53. Is concerned about appearance	4	3	2	1	0	blank
54. Intellectual functioning appears to be at average or above average level	4	3	2	1	0	blank

	Almost Always	Often	Sometimes	Rarely or Never	Insuf. Info.	Not Applicable
Performs well as:						
55. spouse	4	3	2	1	0	blank
56. homemaker	4	3	2	1	0	blank
57. parent	4	3	2	1	0	blank
58. wage earner	4	3	2	1	0	blank
59. member of community	4	3	2	1	0	blank
Derives satisfaction from being:						
60. spouse	4	3	2	1	0	blank
61. homemaker	4	3	2	1	0	blank
62. parent	4	3	2	1	0	blank
63. wage earner	4	3	2	1	0	blank
64. member of community	4	3	2	1	0	blank

Older Child(ren) (10 and over)* (15)

	Almost Always	Often	Sometimes	Rarely or Never	Insuf. Info.	Not Applicable
65. Has been involved in minor law violations	1	2	3	4	0	blank
66. Has been involved in more serious conflicts with law	1	2	3	4	0	blank

*Items refer to one child or several children in the age group.

	Almost Always	Often	Sometimes	Rarely or Never	Insuf. Info.	Not Applicable
67. Has engaged in deviant social behavior (drinking, drugs, sexual, etc.)	1	2	3	4	0	blank
68. Acting-out behavior is normal for age	4	3	2	1	0	blank
69. Appears to have positive self-image	4	3	2	1	0	blank
70. Emotional health appears to be good	4	3	2	1	0	blank
71. Gets along well with most adults	4	3	2	1	0	blank
72. Appears to perform below mental capacity	1	2	3	4	0	blank
73. Appears to perform up to level of physical capacity	4	3	2	1	0	blank
74. Is satisfied with life	4	3	2	1	0	blank
75. Performs household or other duties expected of him/her	4	3	2	1	0	blank
76. School work approximates ability	4	3	2	1	0	blank
77. Positive attitude toward learning	4	3	2	1	0	blank
78. Is a "loner" or withdrawn	1	2	3	4	0	blank
79. Gets along well with friends	4	3	2	1	0	blank

card $\frac{2}{1}$ 2 3 4 5

	Almost Always	Often	Sometimes	Rarely or Never	Insuf. Info.	Not Applicable
Younger Child(ren) (1–9) (14)*						
6. Has been involved in minor law violations	1	2	3	4	0	blank
7. Has engaged in deviant social behavior (aggressiveness, destructiveness, etc.)	1	2	3	4	0	blank
8. Acting-out behavior is normal for age	4	3	2	1	0	blank
9. Appears to have positive self-image	4	3	2	1	0	blank
10. Emotional health appears to be good	4	3	2	1	0	blank
11. Gets along well with most adults	4	3	2	1	0	blank
12. Appears to perform below mental capacity	1	2	3	4	0	blank
13. Appears to perform up to level of physical capacity	4	3	2	1	0	blank
14. Is satisfied with life	4	3	2	1	0	blank
15. Is helpful around the house or with other duties expected of him or her	4	3	2	1	0	blank

*Items refer to one child or several children in the age group.

	Almost Always	Often	Sometimes	Rarely or Never	Insuf. Info.	Not Applicable
16. School work approximates ability	4	3	2	1	0	blank
17. Positive attitude toward learning	4	3	2	1	0	blank
18. Is a loner or withdrawn	1	2	3	4	0	blank
19. Gets along well with friends	4	3	2	1	0	blank

Care and Training of Children

Physical Care (6)

	Almost Always	Often	Sometimes	Rarely or Never	Insuf. Info.	Not Applicable
20. Children have enough to eat	4	3	2	1	0	blank
21. Meals are nutritious	4	3	2	1	0	blank
22. Meals served with regularity	4	3	2	1	0	blank
23. Children have enough clothing	4	3	2	1	0	blank
24. Appropriate supervision of children's activities to prevent physical injury	4	3	2	1	0	blank
25. Health needs are looked after promptly and appropriately	4	3	2	1	0	blank

Training Methods and Emotional Care (9)

	Almost Always	Often	Sometimes	Rarely or Never	Insuf. Info.	Not Applicable
26. Parent(s) reject child(ren)	1	2	3	4	0	blank
27. Parent(s) overly rigid	1	2	3	4	0	blank

	Almost Always	Often	Sometimes	Rarely or Never	Insuf. Info.	Not Applicable
28. Parent(s) overly permissive	1	2	3	4	0	blank
29. Parent(s) expect too much	1	2	3	4	0	blank
30. Parent(s) expect too little	1	2	3	4	0	blank
31. Parent(s) show affection for child(ren)	4	3	2	1	0	blank
32. Discipline is appropriate to behavior	4	3	2	1	0	blank
33. Parents disagree on disciplining children	1	2	3	4	0	blank
34. Mother and father share in "bringing up" children	4	3	2	1	0	blank

Social Activities

Informal Associations (9)

	Almost Always	Often	Sometimes	Rarely or Never	Insuf. Info.	Not Applicable
35. Family gets along with wife's family	4	3	2	1	0	blank
36. Family gets along with husband's family	4	3	2	1	0	blank
37. Family members have friends	4	3	2	1	0	blank
38. Family gets along with neighbors	4	3	2	1	0	blank
39. Family keeps to itself	1	2	3	4	0	blank
40. Husband is satisfied with way he spends leisure time	4	3	2	1	0	blank

	Almost Always	Often	Sometimes	Rarely or Never	Insuf. Info.	Not Applicable
41. Wife is satisfied with way she spends leisure time	4	3	2	1	0	blank
42. Children satisfied with way they spend leisure time	4	3	2	1	0	blank
43. Family in disagreement about how leisure time is spent (e.g., wife dislikes husband's frequent nights out; children disagree on amount of involvement for themselves and/or parents)	1	2	3	4	0	blank

Formal Associations (5)

	Almost Always	Often	Sometimes	Rarely or Never	Insuf. Info.	Not Applicable
44. Family members participate in organized groups (community, union, church, recreational, business, professional, political, special interests)	4	3	2	1	0	blank
45. Husband satisfied with degree/nature of involvement	4	3	2	1	0	blank
46. Wife satisfied with degree/nature of involvement	4	3	2	1	0	blank
47. Children satisfied with degree/nature of involvement	4	3	2	1	0	blank
48. Other household members satisfied with degree/nature of involvement	4	3	2	1	0	blank

Economic Practice

Source of Income (7)

	Almost Always	Often	Sometimes	Rarely or Never	Insuf. Info.	Not Applicable
49. Income derived from work of family members	4	3	2	1	0	blank
50. Income derived from general assistance or other welfare grants	1	2	3	4	0	blank
51. Family able to save money	4	3	2	1	0	blank
52. Family can afford basic necessities	4	3	2	1	0	blank
53. Family can afford at least a few luxuries	4	3	2	1	0	blank
54. Husband satisfied with income	4	3	2	1	0	blank
55. Wife satisfied with income	4	3	2	1	0	blank

Job Situation (3)

	Almost Always	Often	Sometimes	Rarely or Never	Insuf. Info.	Not Applicable
56. Husband has regular employment	4	3	2	1	0	blank
57. Husband satisfied with job	4	3	2	1	0	blank
58. If wife employed, wife satisfied with job	4	3	2	1	0	blank

Money Management (5)

	Almost Always	Often	Sometimes	Rarely or Never	Insuf. Info.	Not Applicable
59. Budgeting haphazard	1	2	3	4	0	blank
60. Impulsive spending	1	2	3	4	0	blank

	Almost Always	Often	Sometimes	Rarely or Never	Insuf. Info.	Not Applicable
61. Money management good	4	3	2	1	0	blank
62. If debts present, payments on debts are met	4	3	2	1	0	blank
63. Husband and wife agree on allocation of money	4	3	2	1	0	blank

Home and Household Practices (8)

Physical Facilities

	Almost Always	Often	Sometimes	Rarely or Never	Insuf. Info.	Not Applicable
64. Apartment or house kept in good condition	4	3	2	1	0	blank
65. Family members appear satisfied with condition and size of home	4	3	2	1	0	blank
66. Family appears satisfied with household equipment and furnishings	4	3	2	1	0	blank
67. Other homes and apartment buildings kept in good condition (repairs, painting, etc.)	4	3	2	1	0	blank
68. Neighborhood kept free of garbage and litter	4	3	2	1	0	blank
69. Sidewalks and streets kept in good repair	4	3	2	1	0	blank

	Almost Always	Often	Sometimes	Rarely or Never	Insuf. Info.	Not Applicable
70. It is safe to walk the streets alone in the neighborhood	4	3	2	1	0	blank
71. Family appears to like neighborhood	4	3	2	1	0	blank
Household Practices (5)						
72. Husband and wife agree on allocation of household chores and tasks (e.g., neither feels overworked or put upon)	4	3	2	1	0	blank
73. Wife finds household chores a drudgery	1	2	3	4	0	blank
74. Housekeeping standards conducive to good health and hygiene	4	3	2	1	0	blank
75. Vermin or rats present in apartment or house	1	2	3	4	0	blank
76. Attention paid to making home attractive and pleasant	4	3	2	1	0	$\frac{3}{1}$ 2 3 4 5 blank
Health Conditions and Practices						card
Health Conditions (3)						
6. Physical health of child(ren) good	4	3	2	1	0	blank
7. Physical health of parent(s) good	4	3	2	1	0	blank

	Almost Always	Often	Sometimes	Rarely or Never	Insuf. Info.	Not Applicable
8. Physical health of one or both parents so poor interferes with ability to function adequately	1	2	3	4	0	blank
Health Practices (7)						
9. Medical care obtained in case of emergency or illness	4	3	2	1	0	blank
10. Preventive medical care obtained	4	3	2	1	0	blank
11. Medical instructions followed	4	3	2	1	0	blank
12. Keep medical or dental appointments	4	3	2	1	0	blank
13. Dental care obtained in case of emergency (toothache, dental injury)	4	3	2	1	0	blank
14. Preventive dental care obtained	4	3	2	1	0	blank
15. Hygiene practices conducive to good physical and dental health	4	3	2	1	0	blank
Relationship with Intervention Worker (if applicable)						
Attitude (2)						
16. Family is friendly to social worker	4	3	2	1	0	blank
17. Family keeps appointments with worker	4	3	2	1	0	blank

	Almost Always	Often	Sometimes	Rarely or Never	Insuf. Info.	Not Applicable
Use of Worker (2)						
18. Family discussed problems freely with social worker	4	3	2	1	0	blank
19. Family takes initiative in seeking help with problems from social worker	4	3	2	1	0	blank
Use of Community Resources						
School (2)						
20. Parents express concern and interest in child(ren's) education	4	3	2	1	0	blank
21. Parents are uncooperative with school in plans for child(ren)	1	2	3	4	0	blank
Religious Institutions (2)						
23. Family derives satisfaction from church or synagogue affiliation or attendance	4	3	2	1	0	blank
24. Religious affiliation or practices are divisive elements in family life	1	2	3	4	0	blank

	Almost Always	Often	Sometimes	Rarely or Never	Insuf. Info.	Not Applicable
Health Resources (2)						
25. Family manifests positive attitudes toward health agencies/resources	4	3	2	1	0	blank
26. Available health facilities are used promptly when need arises	4	3	2	1	0	blank
Social Agencies (2)						
27. Family manifest positive attitude toward social agencies (probation, housing, employment, casework, etc.)	4	3	2	1	0	blank
28. If family has need for services of agency(ies) it utilizes them	4	3	2	1	0	blank
Recreational Agencies (2)						
29. Children use recreational facilities—playgrounds, park, other public facilities	4	3	2	1	0	blank
30. Adults use recreational facilities	4	3	2	1	0	blank

Bibliography

Ackerman, Nathan W. *The Psychodynamics of Family Life, Diagnosis and Treatment of Family Relationships.* New York: Basic Books, 1958.

Andrews, Frank M., and Whithey, Stephen B. *Social Indicators of Well-Being.* New York: Plenum Press, 1976.

Arensberg, Conrad M., and Kimball, Solon T. "Community Study: Retrospect and Prospect." *American Journal of Sociology* 73 (May 1968): 691–705.

289

Axinn, June, and Levin, Herman. *Social Welfare—A History of the American Response to Need.* New York: Dodd, 1975.

Bauer, Raymond A. (a) "Detection and Anticipation of Impact: The Nature of the Task." In *Social Indicators,* edited by Bauer, Raymond; pp. 1-67. Cambridge, Massachusetts: Massachusetts Institute of Technology Press, 1966.

Bauer, Raymond A. (b), ed. *Social Indicators.* Cambridge, Massachusetts: Massachusetts Institute of Technology, 1966.

Beck, Dorothy Fahs. "Research Findings on the Outcomes of Marital Counseling." *Social Casework* 56 (March 1975); 153-181.

Beck, Dorothy Fahs, and Jones, Mary Ann. *Progress and Family Problems.* New York: Family Association of America, 1973.

Beck, Dorothy Fahs, and Jones, Mary Ann. "A New Look at Clientele and Services of Family Agencies." *Social Casework* 55 (December 1974): 589-599.

Behling, John H. "An Experimental Study to Measure the Effectiveness of Casework Services." Unpublished Ph.D. dissertation, Ohio State University, 1961.

Bell, Norman W., and Vogel, Ezra. *A Modern Introduction to the Family.* Glencoe, Illinois: Free Press, 1960.

Bergin, Allen E., and Garfield, Sol L. *Handbook of Psychotherapy and Behavior Change.* New York: Wiley, 1971.

Berleman, William C.; Seaberg, James; and Steinburn, Thomas W. "The Delinquency Prevention Experiment of

the Seattle Atlantic Street Center: A Final Evaluation."
Social Service Review 46 (September 1972): 323-346.

Blood, Robert, and Wolfe, Donald M. *Husbands and Wives.*
New York: Free Press, 1965, pp. 253-255.

Boehm, Werner W. *Objectives of the Social Work Curriculum of
the Future,* Volume 1. New York: Council on Social Work
Education, 1959.

Booth, Charles. *Life and Labour of the People in London.* Re-
printed from the edition of 1902-1904. New York: AMS
Press, 1970.

Bredemeier, Harry C. "The Socially Handicapped and the
Agencies: A Market Analysis." In *Mental Health of the
Poor: New Treatment Approaches for Low Income People,*
edited by Riessman, Frank; Cohen, Jerome; and Pearl,
Arthur, pp. 88-109. New York: Free Press, 1964.

Brim, Orville G.; Fairchild, Roy W.; and Borgatta, Edgar F.
"Relations Between Family Problems." In *Sourcebook on
Marriage and the Family,* edited by Marvin B. Sussman,
pp. 350-367. Boston: Houghton Mifflin, 1963.

Brooks, Thomas R. "Newark." *The Atlantic* 224 (August 1969):
4-12.

Brown, Gordon E., ed. *The Multi-Problem Dilemma.*
Metuchen, New Jersey: Scarecrow Press, 1968.

Buell, Bradley, and associates. *Community Planning for
Human Services.* New York: Columbia University Press,
1952.

Chernick, Jack; Indik, Bernard P.; and Sternlieb, George. *Newark, New Jersey Population and Labor Force.* New Brunswick, New Jersey: Rutgers Institute of Management and Labor Relations, December 1967.

Chilman, Catherine S., ed. *Approaches to the Measurement of Family Change.* Washington, D.C.: U.S. Department of Health, Education, and Welfare, Welfare Administration, June 1966.

Christensen, Harold T., ed. *Handbook of Marriage and the Family.* Chicago: Rand McNally, 1964.

Coulton, Claudia J., and Solomon, Phyllis L. "Measuring Outcomes of Intervention." *Social Work Research and Abstracts* 13 (Winter 1977): 3-9.

Davis, Kingsley. *Human Society.* New York: Macmillan, 1948.

Epstein, Laura. "How to Provide Social Services with Task-Centered Methods—Report of the Task Centered Service Project. Volume I." Mimeographed. Chicago: University of Chicago, School of Social Service Administration, 1977.

Fischer, Joel. "Is Casework Effective? A Review." *Social Work* 18 (January 1973): 5-20.

Fischer, Joel, ed. *The Effectiveness of Social Casework.* Springfield, Illinois: Charles C Thomas, 1976.

Fischer, Joel. *Effective Casework Practice.* New York: McGraw-Hill, 1978.

Flax, Michael, A. *A Study in Comparative Urban Indicators: Conditions in 18 Large Metropolitan Areas.* Washington, D.C.: Urban Institute, 1972.

Freeman, Howard E., and Sheldon, Eleanor Bernet. "Social Indicators." In *Encyclopedia of Social Work—Seventeenth Issue*. Washington, D.C.: National Association of Social Workers, 1977, pp. 1350-1355.

Geismar, Ludwig L. "Family Functioning as an Index of Need for Welfare Services," *Family Process* 3 (March 1964): 99-113.

Geismar, Ludwig L. "The Concept of Community Functioning in Social Work." *Journal of Jewish Communal Service* 42 (Spring 1966): 227-233.

Geismar, Ludwig L. "The Results of Social Work Intervention: A Positive Case." *American Journal of Orthopsychiatry* 38 (April 1968): 444-456.

Geismar, Ludwig L. *Preventive Intervention in Social Work.* Metuchen, New Jersey: Scarecrow Press, 1969.

Geismar, Ludwig L. "Implications of a Family Life Improvement Project." *Social Casework* 52 (July 1971): 455-465.

Geismar, Ludwig L. *555 Families—A Social-Psychological Study of Young Families in Transition.* New Brunswick, New Jersey: Transaction Books, 1973.

Geismar, Ludwig L., and Ayres, Beverly. *Patterns of Change in Problem Families.* St. Paul, Minnesota: Family Centered Project, 1959.

Geismar, Ludwig L., and Ayres, Beverly. *Measuring Family Functioning, A Manual on a Method for Evaluating the Social Functioning of Disorganized Families.* St. Paul, Minnesota: Family Centered Project, 1960.

Geismar, Ludwig L., and Charlesworth, Stephanie. "Parsimonious Practice Research or Have Your Diagnosis and Research It Too." *Australian Social Work* 29 (June 1976): 3-9.

Geismar, Ludwig L., and Geismar, Shirley. *Families in an Urban Mold.* New York: Pergamon Press, 1979.

Geismar, Ludwig L., and Krisberg, Jane. *The Forgotten Neighborhood.* Metuchen, New Jersey: Scarecrow Press, 1967.

Geismar, Ludwig L., and Lagay, Bruce. "Planners' and Consumers' Priorities of Social Welfare Needs." In *Social Work Practice 1965,* pp. 76-95. New York: Columbia University Press, 1965.

Geismar, Ludwig L.; Lagay, Bruce; Wolock, Isabel; Gerhart, Ursula C.; and Fink, Harriet. *Early Supports for Family Life.* Metuchen, New Jersey: Scarecrow Press, 1972.

Geismar, Ludwig, L.; La Sorte, Michael A.; and Ayres, Beverly. "Measuring Family Disorganization." *Marriage and Family Living* 24 (February 1962): 52-60.

Geismar, Ludwig L., and Wolock, Isabel. "Research Data as Aids in Formulating Agency Policy." *Journal of Sociology and Social Welfare* 1 (Fall 1973).

Goode, William J. "The Sociology of the Family." In *Sociology Today,* edited by Merton, Robert K.; Broom, Leonard; and Cottrell, Leonard S. New York: Basic Books, 1959, pp. 17-196.

Grey, Alan L., and Dermody, Helen E. "Reports of Casework Failure." *Social Casework* 53 (November 1972): 534-543.

Gurman, Alan S. "The Effects and Effectiveness of Marital Therapy." *Family Process* 12 (June 1973): 145-170.

Gurman, Alan S. "The Efficacy of Therapeutic Intervention in Social Work: A Critical Evaluation." *Journal of Health and Social Behavior* 15 (June 1974): 136-141.

Heckman, A. A. "Measuring the Effectiveness of Agency Services." *Journal of Social Casework* 29 (December 1948): 394-399.

Hollis, Florence. "Evaluation: Clinical Results and Research Methodology." *Clinical Social Work Journal* 4 (1976): 204-222.

Homans, George C. "Bringing Men Back In." *American Sociological Review* 29 (December 1964): 809-818.

Howe, Michael W. "Casework Self-Evaluation: A Single Subject Approach." *Social Service Review* 48 (March 1947): 1-23.

Hudson, Walter. "Research Training in Professional Social Work Education." *Social Service Review* 52 (March 1978): 116-121.

Hunt, J. McV., and Kogan, Leonard S. *Measuring Results in Social Casework*. New York: Family Service Association of America, 1952.

Jayaratne, Srinika. "Single Subject and Group Designs in Treatment Evaluation." *Social Work Research and Abstracts* 13 (Fall 1977): 35-42.

Jayaratne, Srinika. "Analytic Procedures for Single Subject

296   Family and Community Functioning

Designs." *Social Work Research and Abstracts* 14 (Fall 1978): 30-40.

Kellogg, Paul U. *The Pittsburgh Survey, Volume 1, The Pittsburgh District—Civic Frontage.* New York: Survey Associates, 1914.

Kiresuk, Thomas J., and Lund, Sander. "Goal Attainment Scaling." In *Evaluation of Human Service Programs,* edited by Hargreaves, William A.; Horowitz, Mardi J.; and Sorenson, James E.; pp. 341-370. New York: Academic Press, 1978.

Kiresuk, Thomas J., and Sherman, Robert E. "Goal Attainment Scaling: A General Method for Evaluating Comprehensive Mental Health Programs." *Community Mental Health Journal* 4 (December 1968): 443-453.

Kogan, Leonard, and Shyne, Ann W. "The C.S.S. Movement Scale: A Methodological Review." In *Approaches to the Measurement of Family Change,* edited by Chilman, Catherine S. Washington, D.C.: U.S. Department of Health, Education, and Welfare, Welfare Administration, 1966.

Krupinski, Jersey; Marshall, Elizabeth; and Yule, Valerie. "Patterns of Marital Problems in Marriage Guidance Clients." *Journal of Marriage and the Family* 32 (February 1970): 138-143.

McIntyre, Jennie. "The Structure-Functional Approach to Family Study." In *Emerging Conceptual Frameworks in Family Analysis,* edited by Nye, Ivan F., and Berardo, Felix M. pp. 52-77. New York: Macmillan, 1966.

Mercer, Blaine. *The American Community.* New York: Random House, 1956.

Meyer, Henry J.; Borgatta, Edgar F.; and Jones, Wyatt C. *Girls at Vocational High.* New York: Russell Sage Foundation, 1965.

Moe, Edward O. "Consulting with a Community System: A Case Study." *Journal of Social Issues* 15 (2, 1959): 28-35.

Mullen, Edward J.; Chazin, Robert M.; and Feldstein, David M. "Services for the Newly Dependent: An Assessment." *Social Service Review* 46 (September 1972): 309-322.

Mullen, Edward J., and Dumpson, James R., eds. *Evaluation of Social Intervention.* San Francisco: Jossey-Bass, 1972.

Nover, Leo; Pollak, Carol T.; Robinson, Stephanie G.; and Slawik, Melvin. "A Study of the Social Welfare Needs of the New Brunswick Area." Unpublished M.S.W. thesis. New Brunswick, New Jersey: Rutgers University Graduate School of Social Work, May 1961.

Perlman, Helen Harris. *Social Casework. A Problem-Solving Process.* Chicago: University of Chicago Press, 1957.

Pitts, Jesse. "The Structural-Functional Approach." In *Handbook of Marriage and the Family,* edited by Christensen, Harold T., pp. 51-124. Chicago: Rand McNally, 1964.

Radcliffe-Brown, A. R. *Structure and Function in Primitive Society.* New York: Free Press, 1965.

Reed, Ellery F. "A Scoring System for the Evaluation of Social Casework." *Social Service Review* 5 (June 1931): 214-236.

Reid, William J. "A Test of a Task-Centered Approach." *Social Work* 20 (January 1975): 3–9.

Reid, William J., and Epstein, Laura. *Task-Centered Casework.* New York: Columbia University Press, 1972.

Reid, William J., and Epstein, Laura. *Task-Centered Practice.* New York: Columbia University Press, 1977.

Reid, William, and Shyne, Ann W. *Brief and Extended Casework.* New York: Columbia University Press, 1969.

Reiss, Ira L. "The Universality of the Family: A Conceptual Analysis." *Journal of Marriage and the Family* 27 (November 1965): 443–453.

Riley, Matilda White. *Sociological Research I, A Case Approach.* New York: Harcourt, Brace, and World, 1963.

Rowntree, Benjamin Seebohm. *Poverty: A Study of Town Life.* London: Macmillan, 1902.

Sacks, Joel G.; Bradley, Panke M.; and Beck, Dorothy Fahs. *Clients' Progress Within Five Interviews.* New York: Family Service Association of America, 1970.

Schwartz, Edward E., and Sample, William C. *The Midway Office.* New York: National Association of Social Workers, 1972.

Schwartz, Meyer. "Community Organization." In *Encyclopedia of Social Work,* edited by Lurie, Harry L., pp. 177–190. New York: National Association of Social Workers, 1965.

Segal, Steven Paul. "Research on the Outcome of Social Work Therapeutic Interventions: A Review of the Literature."

Journal of Health and Social Behavior 13 (March 1972): 3-17.

Sheldon, Eleanor Bernert, and Moore, Wilbert E., eds. *Indicators of Social Change.* New York: Russell Sage Foundation, 1968.

Smith, Georgina M. (a) *An Outline of Poverty in Middlesex County.* New Brunswick, New Jersey: Rutgers University Institute of Management and Labor Relations, 1967.

Smith, Georgina M. (b) *On the Welfare.* New Brunswick, New Jersey: Rutgers University Institute of Management and Labor Relations, 1967.

Smith, Mary Lee, and Glass, Gene V. "Meta-Analysis of Psychotherapy Outcome Studies," *American Psychologist* 32 (September 1977) pp. 752-760.

Suchman, Edward A. *Evaluative Research.* New York: Russell Sage Foundation, 1967.

Thomas, Edwin J. "Mousetraps, Developmental Research, and Social Work Education." *Social Service Review* 52 (September 1978): 468-483.

Thomas, Edwin J., and Biddle, Bruce J. *Role Theory: Concepts and Research.* New York: John Wiley and Sons, 1966.

U.S. Department of Commerce. *Social Indicators 1973. Washington, D.C.: U.S. Government Printing Office,* 1973.

U.S. Department of Commerce. *Social Indicators 1976.* Washington, D.C.: U.S. Government Printing Office, 1977.

Wallace, David. "The Chemung County Evaluation of Casework Service to Dependent Multi-Problem Families." *Social Service Review* 41 (December 1967): 379-389.

Wallace, David, and Smith, Jesse. "The Study: Methodology and Findings." In *The Multi-Problem Dilemma,* edited by Brown, Gordon, pp. 107-161. Metuchen, New Jersey: Scarecrow Press, 1968.

Warren, Roland L. *The Community in America.* Chicago: Rand McNally, 1963.

Warren, Roland L. "Toward a Non-Utopian Normative Model of the Community." *American Sociological Review* 35 (April 1970): 219-228.

Whitaker, Ian. "The Nature and Value of Functionalism in Sociology." In *Functionalism in the Social Sciences,* edited by Martindale, Don, Monograph 5, pp. 127-143. Philadelphia: American Academy of Political and Social Science, February 1965.

Wood, Katherine M. "Casework Effectiveness: A New Look at the Research Evidence." *Social Work* 23 (November 1978): 437-458.

Zimbalist, Sidney. *Historic Themes and Landmarks in Social Welfare Research.* New York: Harper and Row, 1977.

Index

FAMILY AND COMMUNITY FUNCTIONING

Second, revised, and expanded edition

LUDWIG L. GEISMAR